COPING

W H E N

A Parent Has

Multiple

Sclerosis

Barbara Cristall

THE ROSEN PUBLISHING GROUP, INC./NEW YORK

Published in 1992 by The Rosen Publishing Group, Inc.
29 East 21st Street, New York, NY 10010

First Edition

Library of Congress Cataloging-in-Publication Data

Cristall, Barbara.
    Coping when a parent has multiple sclerosis / Barbara Cristall.
— 1st ed.
        p.   cm.
    Includes bibliographical references and index.
    Summary: Suggests how to deal with the physical limitations of
the parent who has multiple sclerosis, and how to cope with the
emotional stress that the disease places on the entire family.
    ISBN 0-8239-1406-2
    1. Multiple sclerosis—Juvenile literature. 2. Handicapped
parents—Juvenile literature. 3. Children of handicapped parents—
Juvenile literature. [1. Multiple sclerosis. 2. Physically
handicapped.] I. Title.
RC377.C75   1992
362.1'96834—dc20
                                                    92-14961
                                                    CIP
                                                    AC

Manufactured in the United States of America

To the dearest people in the world, my two sons, Jonathan and Stuart.

ABOUT THE AUTHOR ◇

Barbara Cristall was born in Montreal, Canada. She began doing volunteer work at age sixteen with children at the Jewish General Hospital and later with emotionally disturbed teenagers. She graduated on the Dean's Honor List from Sir George Williams University with a B.A. degree and a major in psychology. After obtaining her teaching credential from Macdonald College of McGill University, she taught grades 1 to 12 for a number of years.

Leaving teaching to become a full-time wife and mother in Edmonton, Alberta, she continued her community work, chairing and organizing many cultural events and fundraisers. She is a founding trustee of The Minerva Foundation and has been on the Board of Directors of various charitable organizations. From 1976 to 1980 she was the producer, interviewer, researcher, and writer of a half-hour television show called "Barbara," dealing with teenage and young adult social problems and issues.

In 1982 Ms. Cristall moved to Beverly Hills, California, where she continued her volunteer work at the Los Angeles County Museum of Art. She was voted Volunteer of the Year for her work with Beverly Hills Arrive Alive, an organization dedicated to educating youth to the hazards of drinking and driving. She is a member of the Board of Directors of Beverly Hills CPR.

This book was developed from a short story Ms. Cristall wrote called "Our Mom Has MS." She is presently working on her second book.

Acknowledgments

My greatest debt is owed to all the people with MS who talked to me and especially to their many children who so openly and honestly shared their experiences. In order to protect their privacy, all names and identifying details have been changed.

I greatly appreciate all the time and energy contributed by my sister, Arlene Levine Krantz, B.Ed., A.A.S., in editing the manuscript.

This book could not have been written without the help and support of:

Louis J. Rosner, M.D., Professor of Neurology UCLA, whose knowledge of MS was a constant invaluable resource.

Stephen C. Reingold, Ph.D., Vice President, Research and Medical Programs, NMSS, who so generously shared his expertise.

Michael Goodman, M.D., whose unique understanding of and experience with teenagers was an enormous help to me.

Audrey Goldman, Director of Chapter Services, NMSS, Southern California Chapter, whose numerous insightful comments and answers to my questions helped to shape the book.

Very special thanks to Rabbi Stephen Robbins and Arnold Gureff, MSW, for their valuable contributions.

Appreciation is also extended to Judith Reichman, M.D.; Kathy Schiff, R.N.; Margaret Calvano, MSLS,

MSIS; Carole Lerner, R.N.; Marshall Berman, M.D.; and Donna Mognett, Ph.D., MFCC, for their helpful input.

I would like to thank my son, Stuart, for encouraging me to start this project; my son, Jonathan, and Alice Hamlett for their countless valuable suggestions; and Frances Thomas, who has been a constant source of support and cheerfully did a variety of tasks not in her job description.

Contents

Introduction

My two sons were teenagers when I received my diagnosis of multiple sclerosis. In this introduction, I would like to share with you some of what I have undergone and learned since then. I hope my experiences and attitude toward life can help you and your family. In addition, I feel confident that this book will help you deal with the challenge of having a parent with MS.

In 1985 the doctor who examined me turned pale when he tapped my right foot with his reflex hammer and it shook back and forth uncontrollably. His immediate and unnecessary comment was, "Go to a neurologist right away—you may be dying from a brain tumor!"

For the next three weeks, until I received the MS diagnosis, I thought I was going to die at any moment, and as a result had a constant, severe headache. After the neurologist had analyzed the results of my MRI and spinal tap and said, with a caring attitude, "You have multiple sclerosis," I felt relief: I wasn't dying after all, and I even thought, "Is that all?" But you have no idea of the anguish I suffered during the next few years as I gradually lost abilities I had had since early childhood.

Because I was trying a variety of self-help methods to arrest the MS, I was open to suggestions from others. If something seemed reasonable, I tried it. My limit was six months. If there was no improvement by then, I moved on to something else.

As my condition worsened, I tried to keep as positive an attitude as possible, but I was not always successful. In fact, in the back of my mind I often saw a wheelchair. Does the mind play some role in affecting the body? I don't know. But much current thinking suggests a mind-body connection.

How did I deal with all this? My neurologist's nurse wrote in a letter to me a while ago, " . . . what I've admired about you these past few years is that despite any initial reluctance or resistance you might feel (and fear) when faced with a new challenge, you always meet it head-on and do beautifully . . . I admire your strength and fighting spirit."

I have a variety of interests and keep very busy. I volunteer time in my community and go to a monthly MS support group. I am fortunate in having some wonderful friends and usually schedule one lunch date a week, because dressing up and being with people I enjoy always lifts my spirits. I travel about in a scooter, which gives me a real feeling of independence (I can move faster than others can walk!). If I have to go far, I take a taxi. The scooter comes apart and fits into a station wagon, but since it is heavy, I also have a twenty-five-pound collapsible wheelchair that fits into any car. My friends can easily lift it when we go places together.

I don't allow myself the luxury of thinking of the past, filled with many happy hours of tennis, jogging, aerobic dancing, and scuba diving; a time when my body always did everything I asked of it. Now I must do daily exercises and treatments to keep as agile and healthy as possible. Most days I also walk twenty feet with my walker, so my body won't forget what it's supposed to be doing. I eat wisely and enjoy a glass of wine each evening with dinner. During the day I drink iced black coffee, which gives me energy.

Because I experience a little fatigue and physically am not very strong, I never expend precious energy unnecessarily. I conserve it for things that are really important. Anything physically demanding (like opening a heavy door), I don't even attempt, but immediately ask for help. I have found, much to my surprise (because I live in California where everyone is, ideally, healthy), that even total strangers have always been marvelous to me and help with anything they can.

Although I have a very full appointment book and do make many long-range plans, I live one day at a time and deal with it as a separate entity, entirely unrelated to yesterday or tomorrow.

To help keep my brain sharp, I read *Time* magazine each week and occasionally *The Journal of Art*, *National Geographic*, and *Departures* (a magazine about exotic places). But sometimes I just do nothing but listen to 'sixties rock-'n'-roll music and hold my cat. Harlequin, who is Siamese and very intelligent and affectionate, is my constant companion. At bedtime, just as my head hits the pillow, he confidently walks into my arms and remains there until morning.

In spite of the many positive aspects of my life, I sometimes get totally depressed for a few days. When that happens, I go with the feeling because I know it's a necessary process. However, if I'm still feeling down after three or four days, I get on the phone and talk to someone caring to help me change my mood. That usually works, but if it doesn't, I see a psychotherapist. After the depression lifts, I always remind myself that it takes both rain and sunshine to make a rainbow.

Religion is very important to me. Although I'm not especially observant, I do attend a weekly class. My spiritual connection to God is steadily increasing in depth and strength, and I pray daily.

Ever since my diagnosis, I've continually asked clergymen, "Why me? What did I ever do to deserve MS?" No one had ever given me an answer I was content with until a few months ago. A very learned, spiritual clergyman replied, "It's not up to us to question what God does. If we could understand the answers, we would be all-knowing, which of course, we aren't. God is good; whatever He does is for the good in the long run." Although that may not seem a satisfactory answer to some people, it's one I can comfortably deal with, and it has given me a large measure of peace. I've stopped questioning and now count my blessings.

Occasionally my sons, Stuart and Jonathan, have disappointed me in how they've dealt with my MS. At other times, I've been very pleasantly surprised. As they've grown older, they've developed greater empathy, and whenever I've needed them for something really important, they've always been there for me. I know from experience that young people must move on with their own lives. I hope that I have had a positive and lasting effect on their characters and personalities.

My most prized possessions are poems they wrote for me, which are framed and hanging above my bedroom desk. Stuart wrote his just after I told my sons of the MS diagnosis:

> When bad things happen to good people
> One thing you can do is pray
> Another thing is to cherish each moment
> As it passes every day
> And try to believe that everything
> Always happens for a reason

Remember tomorrow's a brand-new day
And things can always get better
So when you feel like you just can't go on
And you feel like you can't cope
The water that's more important than
The fountain of youth
Is the magical spring of hope.

Jonathan wrote his poem a few years later:

Birth, Blossoming, she's always a Woman
Marriage, sons & hurt always a Woman
Divorce & Pain still holding strong
      All the People that have hurt her she gives them
her love and forgives
      This woman is my mom: Who always stands up
and gives it her all. And when she falls she gets right
back on her feet.
      My beautiful mom does not know the word
retreat!

I believe fervently, with every fiber of my being, that
somehow, someway, I will walk again. I don't know when
or how it will occur. Maybe it will be from an MS cure or
a clinical trial I'm involved in, or perhaps from some
nonmedical treatment I haven't tried yet. I just feel, deep
within me, that I'm going to live a long, long time, have
many wonderful experiences, and at some point walk
again. I can hardly wait . . .

CHAPTER 1

What Is Multiple Sclerosis?

If your parent has just been diagnosed with multiple sclerosis, you may be feeling frightened and a bit bewildered by the news. It's a shock, and not a pleasant one. You may feel like running away from the problem, perhaps burying yourself under the covers of your bed. Maybe you want to sit and cry, or talk about it with someone you trust. The MS diagnosis may bring on many different feelings, and it's very important to get those feelings out. No matter how you're reacting, no matter how you're feeling, it's normal. You may feel alone with your new fears and concerns, but other young people in your situation share your feelings.

Whatever your reaction is, accept it, as long as it is honest and belongs to you. You may need time alone to think about what the news means to you and your family. A diagnosis of MS creates a major adjustment for everyone. Roles and priorities change, and things are out of kilter for a while. For example, if your parent with MS is the wage earner in your household, it may mean readjustments in time, energy, and function for both your parents. There may also be financial difficulties. Medical visits, nursing care, and aids to help movement may use up a lot of your family's resources. Community financial resources are sometimes available to help families. Your MS Society chapter might know if there are any in your area. Whatever the problems are, though, your family will learn to deal with them. This book will answer many of your questions and offer suggestions to make your life easier.

The first thing to realize is that the arrival of MS in your household will probably create tension and stress because of the unpredictable nature of the disease. If your parents seem angry or depressed, it is most likely because they are having trouble dealing with the diagnosis. It probably has nothing to do with you. If they are preoccupied while they get used to the news, try not to take it personally. They may not have as much time for you as in the past, or they may be short-tempered. That doesn't mean that they love you less, but just that they have other priorities at the moment.

Some parents are very open and want their children to know exactly what is happening to them. Then, of course, it is easy to approach them with questions. Other parents are more private and prefer not to share their personal situation with anyone, even their offspring. If your parents are like that, you'll have to be more assertive and tell them how important it is for you, as a member of the family, to know exactly what is going on. Remind them that you are suffering also, that the MS is affecting you as well as them. If your parents still won't open up, you'll have to seek other sources of information. This book is a good starting point. Perhaps an aunt or an uncle, a teacher or a school counselor can help by talking to your parents on your behalf.

You probably have a lot of questions about MS. If your parents are unable or unwilling to answer them, you can get in touch with the nearest MS Society chapter on your own. The Society provides information, education, and special help for people with MS and their families. The addresses and telephone numbers of offices in the United States and Canada are listed in the Appendix. You can write or telephone them, even toll-free. In the United States, by dialing 1 (800) LEARN MS, you can reach the head office in New York without a long-distance charge. In Canada the toll-free number is 1 (800) 268-7582. Phone at any time, give your name and address, and ask for information about multiple sclerosis. You can also request the address and phone number of your nearest chapter. Confidentiality is a high priority with the Society, and if you wish, the information will be sent to you in an unmarked envelope. The accompanying letter will request that you call again within two weeks if you do not want your name and address sent to your local chapter.

After you have done everything you can to get information and your parents are still reluctant to talk to you, try approaching them again with some MS facts. Let them know that you understand what is going on and want to be involved. Perhaps they will realize that you are sincere and be willing to discuss the MS once you have demonstrated independence in tracking down information. Do your best to get truthful, complete answers to all your questions.

Usually, the doctor who has diagnosed the disease can provide a lot of information. Before you meet with the doctor, read as much as you can about the disease and prepare some questions. Be sure to take a pencil and paper so you can make notes of his answers. When you get home you can read them to your family and discuss any issues of concern.

It is impossible to predict the course of the disease because each MS case is different. Some people have great difficulty walking whereas others have very few symptoms. No matter what the physical condition of your parent, the MS will not necessarily get worse. As a matter of fact, the symptoms may completely disappear.

You cannot inherit MS, nor is it contagious. You can kiss your parent as often as you like and drink from the same cup. Your other parent will not catch the disease either.

Multiple sclerosis is not fatal, although some of its most serious symptoms may be life-threatening if they are not handled properly. In "There Are Lots of Us Out Here," Dr. Labe Scheinberg, professor of neurology, psychiatry, and rehabilitation medicine at Albert Einstein College of Medicine, says that people with MS live almost as long as people without the disease. "As a result of better medical care, the life expectancy is now about 93 percent of normal."[1]

Doctors are unsure whether MS appeared from nowhere in the 1830s or was an older illness that had been overlooked. According to Louis J. Rosner, M.D., and Shelly Ross, in *Multiple Sclerosis*,[2] the symptoms of the disease were first reported by two doctors (one in Paris, the other in London), who independently wrote about a "new" disease. Multiple sclerosis was discovered during

---

[1] "There Are Lots of Us Out Here," in *INSIDE MS*, Winter 1987 (New York: National Multiple Sclerosis Society), p. 21.
[2] Rosner, Louis J., M.D., and Ross, Shelly. *Multiple Sclerosis* (New York: Prentice Hall Press, 1987), pp. 2–4.

autopsies when spots were observed in the central nervous system. In 1867, MS was first reported in America. The illness was not named, but the symptoms described a disease that was obviously MS. It was not until 1878 that the term "sclerosis" first appeared in American medical literature.

SYMPTOMS OF MULTIPLE SCLEROSIS

Today an estimated 250,000 Americans have multiple sclerosis. It is interesting that twice as many women as men have the disease and that whites are affected twice as often as blacks. Nearly 200 new cases are diagnosed each week. The people who have MS probably spent their first fifteen years in a cold climate, and the symptoms usually appear between the ages of fifteen and fifty. These people, some in the prime of life, have symptoms ranging from blurred vision to complete paralysis, and there is no cure.

Not everyone with MS has the same physical problems, and these can change or even disappear. But they sometimes come back. Symptoms are widely varied. One is a prickling in the arms and legs; it is like having a foot go to sleep, but it does not go away as fast. Some people have blurred vision or double vision. Occasionally they lose their balance and fall, or they may drop things. Sometimes people have trouble remembering or speaking, or even doing simple things like reading or writing. Some people have bladder or bowel trouble. And some people have "invisible" MS: They look fine but have symptoms you can't see, like pain or frequent fatigue.

MS affects the brain and spinal cord, which together make up the central nervous system. The central nervous system controls most of the movements and functions of the body. Messages from the brain travel down the spinal cord and along the nerves to the muscles in the part of the body that is supposed to move. For example, if your brain decides you should run, it sends a message to your feet.

The nerve fibers in the brain and spinal cord are covered by a soft, white fatty substance called *myelin*. The myelin insulates the nerves and helps the messages travel efficiently from the brain to the muscles. In MS, areas of myelin are destroyed at irregular intervals (called de-myelination) and are replaced by scar tissue (sclerosed patches). There are many such patches of scar tissue: Multiple sclerosis means "many scars."

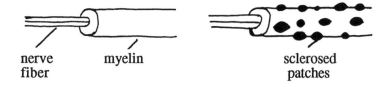

nerve   myelin   sclerosed
fiber   patches

As a result of the demyelination, the speed of the messages, which usually travel up to two hundred miles an hour, is slowed considerably. Movements of the body may become impossible to control because the messages from the brain to the muscles fail to get through correctly—or sometimes at all. Because each person experiences a different pattern of scarring, no two people with MS have exactly the same symptoms.

Remyelination—the ability of the myelin to repair itself —is thought by some doctors to be a possible explanation for remissions. (In remission, the problems or symptoms improve; in exacerbation, they get worse.) The main problem of people with MS is moving properly, but three quarters of them are able to walk (some using aids) even after having the disease for many years.

HOW MULTIPLE SCLEROSIS IS DIAGNOSED

It may have occurred to you that your parent does not really have multiple sclerosis, that the diagnosis was incorrect and perhaps another doctor would find a different, more acceptable disease. That is a possibility, but highly unlikely. Doctors are very careful in diagnosing a serious disease like MS. However, your parents may want to get a second opinion.

You're probably curious about the procedure used to diagnose your parent's multiple sclerosis. You may remember him or her having a number of unusual physical difficulties. According to Margaret Calvano and Barbara Giesser, M.D., in "Diagnosis . . . The Whole Story,"[3] these symptoms may have been very elusive and may have included: unusual fatigue, tingling sensations, numbness in an arm or leg, or slurred speech. Perhaps your parent's symptoms were more severe: " . . . a sudden loss of vision or double vision, bladder incontinence [inability to hold urine], or possibly an overwhelming weakness causing difficulty walking." Whatever the problems were, your parent was probably quite disturbed, made an appointment with the doctor, and was referred to a neurologist, a specialist in diseases of the central nervous system and muscles.

Initially, the neurologist took a thorough medical history, paying particular attention to the symptoms: how often they had occurred, for how long, and whether they

[3] Calvano, Margaret, MSLS, MSIS, Director, Information Resource Center, NMSS, and Giesser, Barbara, M.D., Assistant Professor, Department of Neurology, Albert Einstein College of Medicine, "Diagnosis . . . The Whole Story" in *INSIDE MS*, Summer 1991 (New York: National Multiple Sclerosis Society), pp. 16, 17, 27.

had been constant or had stopped and started. Your parent was also asked about any history of illness or surgeries, whether he or she smoked, drank, or used any drugs, and whether there were any diseases in the family.

Following the medical history, Calvano and Giesser write, your parent had a neurological examination assessing many functional abilities: "one group includes mental, emotional and language functions; the other includes movement and coordination, vision, balance and sensation." During these examinations the doctor observed your parent's conduct, appearance, speed of responding, and clarity of thinking. The doctor also inspected the nerves of the skull. Then the sensory system was examined to determine if your parent could feel "pain, temperature, vibration and position." Your parent's reflexes were also checked with a reflex hammer.

These tests were neither unpleasant nor painful, and the entire examination probably took less than two hours. Calvano and Giesser explain that an accurate diagnosis of MS requires "two attacks at least one month apart, . . . evidence of two separate lesions" (a lesion or plaque is an area where myelin has been destroyed), and no other reason for the symptoms. Occasionally, it is possible for the doctor to diagnose MS from his examination alone, because the indications are so clear.

If testing in addition to the neurological examination is required, Calvano and Giesser write that MRI (magnetic resonance imaging) is "currently the preferred method for imaging the brain to detect the presence of scarring caused by MS. It uses computers and a strong magnetic field to produce pictures of the brain." Although MRI is widely respected, MS cannot be diagnosed exclusively on its outcome. Occasionally people exhibit areas of abnormality on an MRI even though they are perfectly well.

Also, several other illnesses produce brain lesions similar to those of MS. Further, a very few people, diagnosed by other methods as having MS, display no lesions with MRI.

Another test used extensively in MS diagnosis is evoked potential testing, which measures the central nervous system response to stimuli that are quickly and repeatedly presented. It can demonstrate a slowing down of messages in various areas of the nervous system. It complements the MRI, which accurately shows the position of the plaques. The two tests together can assist in making a reliable diagnosis of MS. However, other tests are also helpful in determining whether a person has MS, and your parent's doctor may have decided some of these were indicated. Reaching the diagnosis is not always easy, and the wait can be very difficult for everyone concerned. Some people, however, feel a great sense of relief when they finally know for sure the reason for all the elusive symptoms.

The waiting time, which may be two weeks or more, is a very frightening time. Imaginations run freely and visualize the worst possible outcome. If you remember your parents during this period, they were probably very tense Perhaps you were too. But it is important to remember that a diagnosis of multiple sclerosis is not necessarily a bleak one, because the disease can take different paths. Dr. Labe Scheinberg, collaborating with two colleagues, writes in "MS Overview,"[4] "On an individual basis, disease course and long-term outcome

---

[4] Elkin, Renee, M.D.; Holland, Nancy J., R.N., M.A.; and Scheinberg, Labe, M.D., "MS Overview" (Washington, D.C., copyright 1988, Paralyzed Veterans of America by permission of *Paraplegia News*), pp. 35–36.

cannot be stated with certainty. However, general descriptions can be made:

"The benign course is usually marked by sudden onset of sensory symptoms (e.g., numbness or tingling) or transient temporary loss of vision, with complete or nearly total return to normal. Approximately 20 percent of those with MS will experience a benign course.

"The exacerbating/remitting course generally has a sudden onset of symptoms, followed by partial or total remission. There is often a long period of stability between attacks, sometimes lasting for years. Approximately 20 to 30 percent of persons with MS fall within this category.

"The remitting/progressive course also has a sudden onset of symptoms, which are likely to be weakness, tremor or incoordination. However, degree of recovery diminishes with each attack, so that an overall decline is experienced. About 40 percent of individuals with MS fit this category.

"The progressive course has an insidious [not obvious] onset. There is a steady decrease in function that may plateau at some point or continue until total disability occurs, within many months or years. Ten to 20 percent of MS cases are estimated to be progressive."

Even if you know at any moment which of the above groups your parent is in, it is impossible to predict a long-term course for the disease. It's a "waiting game" because multiple sclerosis affects each person differently.

You already know from experience that waiting is easier if you are busy with something else. After the initial shock of the diagnosis has worn off, your family members will benefit from returning to their regular routines as much as possible. That is not to suggest that you should avoid facing reality, but rather that you should focus on the present with as positive an attitude as possible. Optimism will encourage everyone to put forth their best efforts, and your family will benefit from positive behavior.

RESEARCH AND TREATMENT

Scientists all over the world are engaged in research to discover the cause of MS and how to prevent it, as well as to find better ways of treating the disease. Some of their work seems quite promising.

A disease called experimental allergic encephalomyelitis (EAE) is similar to MS in that both diseases involve demyelination and the formation of scar tissue. Scientists create EAE in rats, mice, and guinea pigs and then use various methods that sometimes create remissions in the animals. Numerous methods of treatment of MS have resulted from this research, and it is hoped that even more effective treatments will be discovered. Scientists in Israel have performed bone marrow transplants from healthy mice to mice with EAE with considerable success. The technique has not been tried in humans because it is invasive and risky, but as additional information is acquired it may turn out to be a possible way to combat MS.

The body's main defense against alien invaders are the T-cells. It is believed that in multiple sclerosis the T-cells malfunction and attack the myelin insulating the nerves. Dr. Howard Weiner and researchers at Brigham and Women's Hospital in Boston believe that myelin protein stops the malfunctioning T-cells from their mistaken attack. Using this theory, these doctors were successful in stopping the progress of EAE in mice who were fed myelin protein. This is a safe treatment, with relatively few side effects. Studies on humans with MS have begun, but it is too soon to know their exact effect.

As we have seen, MS attacks the central nervous system. Researchers have used monoclonal antibodies against certain cells that they believe cause harm to the central nervous system. This treatment has been successful against EAE in mice: The progression of the disease was halted and paralysis was reversed in ninety percent of the animals. Early studies on people with MS have been begun to test the safety of this technique; it is too soon to know whether it is effective.

Total lymphoid irradiation involves X rays aimed at the body's lymph nodes while the rest of the body is well shielded. In a small study, two thirds of the patients (who all had progressive MS) have had no worsening of their condition for up to four years since beginning treatment. The technique may have some negative side effects, but it is being carefully studied in ongoing trials.

More extensive research is required to show whether any of these methods will stop the progression of the disease or prevent exacerbations. How will it all turn out? No one knows. The answer may come from specific research into MS or from research into another neurological ailment entirely. In the meantime, scientists are devoting a great deal of time and energy to the subject. Participation by MS patients in these studies is vital to ensure success. Through this cooperation and ever-expanding technology, a breakthrough will take place and the puzzle of multiple sclerosis will finally be solved.

There are various treatments for MS, and each has its own risks and benefits. Your parent's doctor will probably help to decide which route should be followed. Up to this point more than one hundred treatments have been tried, many of them based on scientific research. Many, however, have no scientific basis and are not really effective. Currently, more than one hundred clinical trials are being conducted in medical centers around the world. Some people believe that even before the cause of MS is found, a way to arrest the disease will be discovered.

New approaches to treatment are constantly being tried, which at present must be considered experimental because they have not been proven. Current clinical trials include drugs that suppress immune system activity (immunosuppressants). Cyclophosphamide (Cytoxan) has been used in combination with ACTH by Dr. Howard Weiner. In some studies, it has succeeded in halting chronic-progressive MS for up to two years in about two thirds of the treated patients. Other studies, however, have not shown such benefit. The major drawback to the treatment is serious side effects. As an immunosuppressant, the drug drastically lowers the white blood cell count, reducing the body's ability to fight infection. Immediate side effects are hair loss and nausea and vomiting. Long-term effects are not known for certain, but there is a possibility of bladder cancer, leukemia, or other complications. Many doctors oppose this treatment because it is so toxic and its benefit is questionable.

For the exacerbating/remitting type of MS, use of Copolymer 1, imported from Israel, resulted in fewer exacerbations in patients treated with the drug as compared with another group receiving a placebo (an inactive substance given to a patient who thinks it is medicine). However, Copolymer 1 does not help chronic-progressive MS. Research in this area is continuing.

Several drugs have had proven success with people who experience flare-ups of MS. Steroids like prednisone and prednisolone or ACTH are often prescribed for severe attacks. They often shorten exacerbations and make them milder, but they do not prevent future attacks and they have no known effect on the long-term course of the disease. Since remissions may occur naturally in the exacerbating/remitting type of MS, an improvement after a treatment does not necessarily mean it was because of the treatment.

Steroids and ACTH operate by decreasing antibody production by the immune system and by reducing the swelling and inflammation of myelin. They are the only quick and scientifically proven way to fight a new attack, and they often help to avoid possible permanent damage. They can be used only for a brief time, as the side effects become progressively severe. In a course of two to six weeks, however, the benefits outweigh the risks. The side effects include increased appetite, weight gain, water retention, puffiness, mood changes, acne, and insomnia.

The various symptoms of multiple sclerosis are dealt with in many ways. A large number of people with MS experience muscle stiffness (spasticity). Drugs and physical therapy may be helpful, although no drug is completely capable of effecting a change. Medication often aids bladder problems, and changing the person's diet may help bowel difficulties. Tremor (shaking) may hinder your parent's ability to carry on with everyday life, and sometimes medication helps. Fatigue can occasionally be eased by drugs. Vision problems (if they do not clear up by themselves) can usually be helped by steroid-type drugs. Your parent may have emotional problems caused by dealing with the diagnosis and may need a referral to a psychologist or psychiatrist.

You can help most by being a good listener. If you find yourself unable to respond directly to your parent's questions or comments, you can still be supportive by caring enough to simply listen. Although your parent is probably very upset, try to remember, and remind your family, that the illness may not progress at all. In fact, your parent may go into complete remission for many years.

ACCEPTANCE

Your parent will go through various stages before coming to terms with the diagnosis of MS. The first stage is one of disbelief, total rejection of the situation. The second stage still involves some nonacceptance, and your parent will fight valiantly against becoming depressed about the diagnosis. Next, your parent will be more receptive of the situation and more realistic about dealing with it directly. Finally, your parent will reach a stage of complete acceptance of the fact that he or she has multiple sclerosis. Arriving at this final acceptance does not mean that your parent won't struggle to maintain his or her independence if new symptoms occur, but a kind of inner peace is achieved.

These stages are particularly difficult to deal with in MS because of the exacerbations and remissions the disease entails. Just as your parent may finally be able to accept the situation, he or she might have an exacerbation and immediately lose the stage of final acceptance and have to go through the stages all over again.

The stages have no time frame. They can take months or even years. Not everyone experiences each one of the stages, and some people go through them in different sequences. You and the rest of your family may go through some of them as well. Be prepared for some disbelief and denial before everyone reaches acceptance. If you feel that a significant length of time has passed and one or more members of your family are still having difficulty accepting the disease, try talking to them to see if you can help them be more receptive. If that fails, suggest that they get professional help. They would probably benefit from talking to someone who is objective and trained to help people cope with difficult situations.

Multiple sclerosis is not an easy illness, but with loving acceptance and courage your family can learn to cope. Many people with MS stay vital and active throughout their lives. They may not even have to change their long-range objectives, but just the way they go about achieving them.

A diagnosis of MS means a new beginning. If you learn to value the beauty of each moment, you will treasure the present and not dwell on the past. Through cooperation and patience, your family unit will grow stronger and you will become a more mature and thoughtful person. Your reaction to the challenge of MS will have a tremendous influence on how you deal with the course of your life. If you meet the challenge with perseverance and optimism, you will emerge a winner.

CHAPTER 2

Your Life *Is* Different

T he chief characteristic of your family's life right now is probably change. Routines that seemed permanent have been upset, and everyone seems to be going in different directions. Your parent who has MS is suddenly the focus of attention, and everything else has been set aside. You may want to scream, to get everyone to behave as they used to, because the diagnosis of MS has suddenly turned your whole world upside down.

Your parents may seem constantly preoccupied with the disease. That is normal. They both may be very frightened. But things will calm down when they get used to the diagnosis.

A serious illness can affect a family in one of two ways. It can make everyone much closer, part of a strong family unit, loving and sharing emotions freely, or everyone can remain isolated in his or her own space and grow further and further apart. If you sense that your family is drifting apart, share your concern with your parents. Explain how isolated you feel and how you really need them. They are probably longing for nurturing and kindness just as you are. Even if they don't respond right away, keep reaching out to them and offering your love and support.

Sometimes family members find that they are arguing all the time. But it is the disease they are angry at, not each other. Vanessa experienced just the opposite: Her parents hardly spoke to each other, but when they did, they used low voices and as few words as possible and seemed angry. They hardly spoke to anyone else in the family. The house was full of tension. What Vanessa didn't know was that before her mother was diagnosed with MS, her parents had been planning to get a divorce. Now her father felt guilty about leaving her mother. Vanessa finally spoke to her parents and told them how difficult it was to live in such a stress-charged atmosphere. They all found it very helpful to talk with a family therapist, who encouraged the divorce, in spite of the MS.

Perhaps your parents seem more united now, like team members working toward a common goal. Mark said, "My parents were practically always together. Mom was constantly puffing up Dad's pillows or tucking in his blanket. She hovered over him like a mother hen. I even saw them whispering secrets to each other, making sure that no one else could hear."

Your parents may emphasize the importance of co-operation and the need for each person to do his part to strengthen the family unit. Monica's parents dealt with their changed life-style this way: "Dad called a group meeting. Mom, Dad, my two younger brothers, and I all went into the family room. Dad started off the meeting by saying that he had something important and serious to tell us. Then he told us about Mom's diagnosis of MS and how concerned he was about her. We discussed the fact that Mom would have to quit her job soon, because the disease made her so tired. That meant we all had to get part-time jobs after school, to earn our own spending money."

The diagnosis of MS may affect your parent in different ways. He or she may choose to deny having the disease by going from doctor to doctor, hoping to get a different diagnosis, or by refusing to wear a necessary brace or use a cane or walker. Or he or she may accept the diagnosis and exhibit anger or grief, which are normal emotions for both your parents. It is perfectly acceptable for everyone in your family to experience conflicting emotions, and it is important to share those feelings.

Crying is a tremendous release of tension for anyone. Patty says, "I did my best to keep from crying when my mother got MS, even though I was so worried because I didn't know what our future would be like. I tried to be brave for my mother's sake but I finally broke down and wept. Mom, who had always had a lot of self-control, began to cry as well. The two of us clung to each other and sobbed for a long, long time. Afterward we felt a great sense of relief."

CHALLENGE OF NEW RESPONSIBILITIES

After the initial diagnosis of MS, your family will feel confused and unsettled. Then gradually everyone will once again become preoccupied with daily needs and obligations. But there will probably be many changes in the family routine. Everyone will have to pitch in and help on a regular basis. You may find that you're in charge of meals, laundry, food shopping, housecleaning, or many other chores.

As a result of the additional responsibility, none of you may have as much free time as before. There may not be as many opportunities to spend quality time alone with your healthy parent. But you can be together and help out at the same time. You can shop and then cook a meal together, or clean the garage. Many chores have to be done, and your parent will welcome your help and the chance to spend time with you.

If you feel overwhelmed, speak out and say what is on your mind. Remember that if your parent with MS is unable to do much, your other parent will be shouldering a double load. If your parents are divorced, each family member will have even more responsibilities. Everyone will have to do more than what you may consider "fair" and will be expected to be fairly cheerful about it as well. However, no one expects you to be phony or to keep a smile on your face at all times.

Above all else, you must be genuine about expressing your emotions. Margo says, "I had a really difficult time. My parents' constant cheerful attitude put a lot of pressure on me. I know they expected me to smile and stay calm, but my stomach was constantly in knots. I finally had to go to my family doctor for medication. I also had to explain to my parents that their forced cheerfulness was placing unfair and unreal expectations on me."

You may feel that a lot of responsibility has been thrust on you and that you're expected to grow up suddenly. Perhaps you have to take care of younger brothers and sisters as well as do chores. Resentment may be building up inside you because you think tasks have not been divided equally and you are expected to do more than your fair share. Try to be objective about the situation. If you believe that your complaint is legitimate, suggest a family meeting and speak maturely about it. Use notes or a list, if that will make it easier. You need to express as clearly as possible any anger or frustration that you're feeling. Jordan became increasingly stressed by not complaining about his older sister's laziness. When he finally expressed his anger and asked his parents why she couldn't pitch in a little more, they agreed that his complaint was justified. As his sister became more cooperative, he felt more relaxed and energetic.

If speaking to your parents is difficult for you, why not explain your problem to an adult they respect. Perhaps this friend can speak to your parents alone or back you up when you're all together.

There is no question that you have to pitch in and help, but your schoolwork should not have to suffer and there should be time each week for friends and relaxation. Nancy says, "I have a lot more chores to do than I used to, but I prioritize and am really organized. I've discovered that after working really hard during the week, I have time to talk on the phone and see my friends on the weekend."

Brian had a different problem: He had to take care of three younger sisters who were always fighting. When his mother was resting and he was alone with them, everything was fine and they listened to him. But when his mother was there she undermined his authority by bossing him around and yelling at his sisters. He was so disturbed by this that he appealed to his father, who helped Brian's mother understand his struggles.

Angie says, "My parents got really overprotective, as if they were afraid I would get sick too. They were stricter than they had been for years; a lot of my newfound independence was suddenly taken away. I was no longer allowed to make my own decisions, and they wouldn't let me spend much time with my friends. It made me angry to be treated like a child again when I was almost grown up. I talked to my guidance counselor at school, and she persuaded my parents to ease up on me."

FINANCIAL CHANGES

If the wage earner in your family has MS and is unable to work, your Social Security office will be able to advise you about benefits that may be available. Because of the changed circumstances in your family, your other parent may have to get a job. That might involve returning to the workforce after an absence of many years and perhaps retraining to bring job skills up to present-day standards. All this takes time and is difficult for everyone involved. If your parents feel overwhelmed by increased expenses, the MS Society can provide counseling to help them adjust to their new situation. Some chapters of the Society have a share-of-cost program that helps people purchase equipment and walking aids. They also occasionally provide wheelchairs and hospital beds on a temporary basis.

Perhaps your parents have friends or family who can give them financial help. You may be surprised at the offers of help that come from unexpected sources. With patience and determination from each family member and some outside help and support, your family will find a way out of their financial difficulties.

With so much income being used for medical expenses, the children may need to get part-time jobs for spending money or to contribute to the family's finances. Remember that your financial help is also a contribution toward family unity and harmony. By helping to improve the situation, you will feel less resentful of the new demands on your time and energy.

If you are too young to get a job or if you need to stay close to home, there are many ways to earn money in your own neighborhood. Perhaps you can mow lawns or rake leaves, shovel snow, clean out your neighbors' attics, or help them paint a room or a fence. Even young teenagers can earn money baby-sitting. You can be a mother's helper for the summer or even for a few hours a day, giving young children baths and reading to them before bed, or tutoring older children. Jason discovered that he had a talent for making children laugh, and his sister, Rachel, enjoyed decorating and setting up for birthday parties. They worked as a team: He dressed up as a clown and did magic tricks, and they both organized games for the children to play.

There are many things you can do to earn money, but you need to make people aware of your services. Ask a friend who is artistic to help you make up a flier describing what you can do. Perhaps someone you know has access to a copy machine and can save you the cost of printing a large number of fliers. Then ring doorbells, introduce yourself, and hand out your fliers. Or you can place them in mailboxes, or on bulletin boards in libraries, community league offices, and grocery stores.

If you're a little older you can get a part-time job after school and on weekends, working in a neighborhood store, pumping gas, or bagging groceries. Even if a store is not advertising for part-time help, you can still ask the manager to keep you in mind if a job opens up.

ILLNESS COMPLICATES ADOLESCENT TURMOIL

Being a teenager is difficult enough without having MS in the family. The addition of the disease really complicates everything. In *The Turbulent Teens*, Dr. James Gardner writes: "Adolescence can be such a confusing time. The teenager's body is changing in bewildering though wonderful ways. Irrational feelings and swings of mood seem to come out of nowhere."[1]

You have already begun the sexual changes, the growth of facial and bodily hair and a deepening voice in males, and menstruation and the growth of breasts and bodily hair in females. You're also going through a time of rapid changes in your needs, attitudes, and interests. You would probably prefer to ignore the responsibilities that are being forced on you. You may be yearning to rebel against them to strengthen your own developing personality. Unfortunately, just as you are feeling the need for increased independence, new demands are being thrust upon you, both at home and at school. So many conflicting forces are interfering with your efforts to carve out an adult identity for yourself.

Many teenagers use withdrawal as a way of dealing with their conflicting emotions. They either withdraw into their bedroom and close the door, or they withdraw psychologically. That is normal. Teenagers must separate from both parents to move from the dependence of childhood to the independence of adulthood. Your parents may help you make this transition without feeling threatened, or they may hold the reins even tighter for fear of letting you go.

It may seem that you have a tough road ahead of you. To achieve the freedom and independence that you want, you have to prove to your parents that you are worthy of increased responsibility, and yet you may be feeling burdened by too much responsibility, too quickly. It is difficult to balance the desire for freedom with respect for

---

[1] Gardner, James, Ph.D. *The Turbulent Teens* (Los Angeles: Sorrento Press, Inc., 1983), p.3.

daily obligations. Your inner turmoil may manifest itself as intense anger toward your parents. Feelings of anger and resentment are a normal outcome of your desire to be independent and to be on an equal footing with your parents.

Another complication in your relationship with your parents may be your growing awareness and criticism of their faults. When you were younger, you probably thought your folks were perfect: understanding, all-knowing, and able to handle any situation. Now your parents may appear helpless and unsure of themselves in the face of MS. They may be spending all their time and energy dealing with this upheaval in their lives and thus appear weak and indecisive. How can you look to them for answers to your difficulties if they cannot solve their own problems?

This is a time for you to understand that your parents are human, with all the needs and pressures that you are also experiencing. If you judge them harshly you will feel alone and separated from them. Reach out to them even if you have no concrete suggestions. Use your emerging independence to reach out and say, "It's okay if you're not sure how to deal with this. I'm old enough to love you even if you don't have all the answers." A loving hug, an unexpected meal prepared, an unasked-for errand run, or a small, thoughtful gift are ways to assert your independence and still help yourself and those around you. You can also assert your independence in a positive way by seeking out adults and friends who will listen to you sympathetically. Remember to ask your friends for help when you feel overwhelmed by extra household tasks. Baby-sitting for your younger siblings will be more fun if you and a friend make popcorn or cookies that everyone can enjoy.

EMOTIONAL CONFLICTS

The three emotions you probably feel as a result of the MS diagnosis are anger, guilt, and helplessness. These emotions are perfectly natural for a person to feel when he or she or a loved one is faced with a serious chronic disease.

Anger is probably the first emotion you will feel. Your whole life has been turned upside down. Things that you once took for granted, like time to see your friends and talk on the phone, may now seem impossible with your new, hectic schedule. Perhaps there isn't even time for that part-time job you enjoyed so much, that made you feel proud to be earning your own money. You're entitled to be angry, but you must find an outlet for your aggressive feelings. If you bury them deep inside, you may lose your temper, avoid your parent who has MS, or blame him or her for all the problems in the family. It is important to talk frankly with everyone in your family so you can understand each other's needs and inner conflicts. That does not mean that shouting and screaming are justified during family rap sessions. Your emotions can be expressed quietly, with a lot of strength behind them.

You may be angry about the chores that force you to sacrifice your favorite activities. Gregg was upset with all the baby-sitting he had to do. His older sister was away at college, and he was left in charge of his younger brother and sister while his mother worked. He had to go home right after school to supervise them, and it seemed totally unfair to him. The kids could still go to baseball practice and he had to take them, but he had to give up playing in the band—there was just no time.

You may feel that your parent has let you down by not being strong and healthy and there for you. Or you may be afraid that something will happen to your other parent. All these feelings are natural. It's perfectly understandable for you to be concerned about your own well-being. You should be; you're as important as anyone else in your family.

Guilt feelings are also normal. You may feel guilty because you would rather have had your healthy parent sick instead. Mike felt especially guilty. He had always been close to his mother and had put her on a pedestal. When she got MS, he secretly wished it had been his dad instead. Perhaps you share Bob's feelings: "The week before the diagnosis, I had been furious with my father and just wished he would stop bothering me. Suddenly he was too sick to pay much attention to me, so I got my wish after all. I felt terrible."

Perhaps you thought your parent was imagining it when he or she complained about blurred vision or feeling tired even after a good night's sleep. Maybe you accused him or her of making it up, and now all you can feel is overwhelming guilt. But how could you have known? Even the doctors didn't know for sure until all the test results were in. You have to be patient and understanding of yourself too and take whatever time you need to adjust to the new situation.

Feeling helpless is a natural reaction when one of your parents has MS. You feel powerless. You may feel angry and frustrated by the uncertainty of MS. Your parent's condition may change daily, making it impossible for your family to make long-range plans. Jamie's father never knew if he would have enough energy to participate in a family outing; sometimes trips had to be canceled at the last minute. Jamie was miserable with this new way of life until someone suggested that she deal with each day separately. That seemed like such a simple solution, and yet, for her, it worked. Now, when her family plans an activity they always have an alternative in case the original plan doesn't work out.

Your desire to be with your ill parent may conflict with his or her needs at a particular moment. Perhaps your parent wants to be alone a lot or, on the contrary, wants someone nearby at all times. Jessica was excited about her science project and thought her father would enjoy sharing it with her. But when she set it up beside his bed, he became annoyed and they began to argue. Finally she realized that he was exhausted and had been planning to take a nap. Jessica felt frustrated and unappreciated, while her father complained that everyone ignored his needs. The whole family benefited from therapy: They learned to tune in to one another so that conflicting needs could be dealt with more effectively. If everyone speaks openly about needs and desires, many difficulties can be resolved with a minimum of stress.

As everyone becomes more accustomed to the disease, you will be more attuned to it and more flexible in response to its fluctuating nature. If you make an effort to speak less and listen more, you will become more sensitive and intuitive to those around you.

Perhaps you are determined that your family, especially your parent with MS, will beat the disease. That's good! Determination and a positive attitude are your best weapons in the fight against multiple sclerosis. Even if you don't see immediate progress, your courage will bolster everyone's spirits. If you strive to do your best and encourage others around you to cooperate, each member will strengthen your family unit.

Social Support Is Important

Now more than ever, you and your parents will value the love and support of good friends. Unfortunately, some people will not live up to your needs and expectations. Just as your parents' friends will either be supportive or not, you'll experience the same situation with your own friends. Some of your friendships will grow stronger while others fall by the wayside. It is almost impossible to predict the future of your relationships; only time will tell.

Some people need to be alone when something upsetting happens in their lives. Others need the company of friends. Each person must work out what is best for him or her. Perhaps, like Peter, you will be uncomfortable with your friends for a while after the diagnosis. Peter was very upset and didn't want to talk to anyone. He couldn't stand their questions. As soon as school was over he walked home alone and became totally involved in his household chores. On the other hand, Alexandra said, "I needed my friends and welcomed their support. They gave me a much needed break from the problems at home. When I was with them, they made me laugh and sometimes forget the sadness that was inside me."

Your friends will probably have a lot of questions about multiple sclerosis; although practically everyone has heard of the disease, most people don't know much about it. Some of the questions may seem silly, but try to be patient and explain as clearly as you can. Your friends truly care about you and are genuinely concerned about the illness and its effects on you.

Although Laura was not uncomfortable answering questions, she found the doings and conversations of her friends suddenly superficial and was inwardly very impatient with them. She could interact honestly with one or two friends, but in a larger group she felt compelled to act carefree even when she actually was miserable.

When your parent initially gets MS, most of your friends will sympathize with you. Later some may tire of the situation and drift away. A few of your friends may be uncomfortable with your new situation and avoid you, making all sorts of excuses for not getting together. There's nothing much you can do in such cases except confront them honestly. If that doesn't work, try to accept the situation and move on. Spend your precious time with friends whom you can trust and respect. You need friends who care enough to be understanding of your demanding situation.

Sometimes you may feel that you're too dependent on your friends, that you are always the one for whom they have to put themselves out. But there are many ways to show how much you appreciate their support. If you're artistic or handy with tools, you can create something beautiful and useful. You can cook or bake something delicious. You can help with chores or run errands for them. Karen was grateful to several friends who were so supportive when she felt overwhelmed by her mother's MS. She wanted to show her appreciation in some tangible way but couldn't figure out what was needed. Finally she asked each friend individually: One wanted help washing the car, one needed inspiration for a science project, and another needed a cake for the school's bake sale. These were things Karen could do well, and she was delighted to repay their kindness. Now she could feel independent again.

John also longed to do something for his friend, David, who was always sharing his burden of errands and chores. But what could John do? He had no spare time to help with David's chores, and he had no extra money to buy him a gift. Finally he had a great idea: David needed help in Math and History, and those were John's best subjects. If they studied together, he could help David without taking extra time from his hectic schedule.

Your Needs Are Important

Now that you are so busy trying to balance schoolwork, extracurricular activities, and all your new household responsibilities, you may forget to take care of yourself. With everyone's time and energy focused on your parent who has MS, the need for you to get plenty of rest and exercise may at first seem trivial or even selfish. You may feel silly thinking about jogging when your family members are worrying about unpaid bills or your parent's illness.

The best way to deal with problems is to strengthen yourself enough to face them. Cathy rented aerobic tapes from the library and exercised three times a week. At first her sisters criticized her and thought she didn't care about their mother. After a few weeks, however, they realized that they were dragging themselves around, too exhausted to do homework or housework. Cathy, on the other hand, was completing her chores, maintaining a B average, and still had time to see her friends. Pretty soon Cathy's sisters were eager to work out with her.

Instead of spending time on the phone or going to the movies with your friends, why not encourage them to go for a long walk or jog or bicycle ride with you? While you're baby-sitting for your siblings, you can make a game out of exercises and gymnastics such as tumbling and cartwheels. It will relieve the boredom, raise your spirits, and energize all of you.

Getting enough rest and exercise is only part of the picture; you must also eat nourishing meals and snacks. It is easy to grab a chocolate bar or a bag of chips when you're starving and feeling blue, but that won't sustain you to carry your fair share of family responsibilities. Your body needs proper fuel—fruits, vegetables, whole grains, proteins, and dairy products—to get you successfully through your hectic days.

Ask the librarian for some simple cookbooks that your whole family can get into together. The Home Economics teacher can probably make some good suggestions for quick, easy, and nutritious meals. Stephen enjoyed cooking but hated cleaning up afterward. His sisters agreed to straighten up after all his "culinary concoctions," and he was free to create delicious, healthful meals. He was amazed at how much he enjoyed food preparation and decided to take cooking classes at the local college one night a week. Ultimately he went on to become a very successful chef, but he never forgot his first teacher's advice: Basic, healthful foods nourish the mind as well as the body.

Although the teenage years are often stormy, you need to strive for balance in your life. You may face some really tough times, but you need to take responsibility for your own welfare as well as meet your obligations to your family. Remember that, even though someone in your family has MS, you are just as important as that someone, and you need to follow positive paths to physical, mental, and emotional well-being.

CHAPTER 3

Positive and Negative Outlets for Stress

COMMUNICATION

Perhaps the tension of having a serious illness in your house is jarring everyone's nerves, and the members of your family are not being honest about their feelings. Communication may be ineffective, creating a feeling of frustration among you. To deal with it in the best way, try to avoid confronting your parents with angry accusations. Organize your thoughts and your suggestions for improving communication by making a list. Then approach them and request an open discussion.

Because of the tension in your home, it will be difficult for everyone to remain calm, but here are some tips that may help you:

- Don't take it for granted that you know your parents' innermost feelings. To communicate with them and understand their point of view, you must listen with a compassionate heart.

- Try to be sympathetic with their point of view even if it differs from yours, and be careful not to belittle them in any way.
- Present your opinion in a straightforward, non-threatening manner. Be sure not to raise your voice; they may do likewise, and issues are difficult to settle when people are attempting to outshout each other.
- Rather than insisting on having your own way, encourage compromise so that, in a sense, each of you can feel like a winner.
- If you are able to agree on some issues, write them down so that you can all experience a sense of accomplishment.

Your discussion may do no more than give everyone an opportunity to be heard, but that in itself can increase family unity.

As a teenager moving toward adulthood, you may be experiencing many conflicting emotions as you strive for independence. The needs of your parent with MS have caused your family to increase its expectations of you; you're suddenly more tied to them than ever before, and it may be hard to deal with the added responsibilities. Perhaps your parents are even treating you like an adult in many ways, and you may have mixed emotions about that. On the one hand, you enjoy and appreciate your new grown-up status and the respect you have achieved. You like it when you express an opinion and your parents really listen to you. Perhaps they even confide in you. And maybe no one bothers you with curfews or seems to care whether you attend school or not. On the other hand, your precious free time is taken up by all the chores you have to do.

Although it's normal for you to feel angry, you need to find the most positive way to deal with your new situation. MS doesn't just go away. Somehow you have to learn to be part of the team supporting your parent. As the disease changes, as it often does, you'll find more space for yourself and life will be less confining. But you will still need to be aware of anger or other negative feelings you are experiencing and express them.

Debbie did not do so and suffered a great deal. She felt ignored, unloved, and unwanted when her mother was diagnosed with MS and her father acted as if she didn't exist. She craved his attention so much that she started to steal from stores as she wandered through them. One day she got caught, and the police telephoned her father. He was furious with her, but when she explained her feelings he suddenly understood. From then on he changed his way of dealing with Debbie and the illness.

One of the emotions you may feel is fear. When we're small, we get used to having our parents take care of us, and now you suddenly have one parent sick and the other too busy to pay much attention to you. You may wonder who will take care of you if you need help. It's perfectly natural to worry about yourself. But your parents do care about you even though they seem preoccupied with their own worries. If you reach out to them, they will respond.

You may even worry that you'll get multiple sclerosis too. Not enough is known about the disease to be able to predict who will get it and who won't. Children with a parent who has MS have a slightly (*very* slightly) greater chance of acquiring the disease. The best way to deal with this fear is to take care of yourself physically by eating well and exercising, and mentally by keeping your mind active and stimulated and by choosing positive ways to deal with stress.

NEED FOR EMOTIONAL SUPPORT

As a result of all the time MS is demanding from your parents, you may find that you're on your own too much. If talking to them about it has not helped, speak to a teacher you like or a school counselor. Almost every high school and college has at least one counselor who is trained to deal with students' personal problems. A counselor can help you organize your free time and even suggest some books that can help you plan your days.

It's easy to get into trouble if you have a lot of unstructured time on your hands. Frances mistakenly believed that since her parents didn't pay much attention to what she did, they didn't care. So she began to skip school when she felt like it and go to the movies. The principal discovered what was going on and called her parents to a conference at school. They concluded that Frances had had far too much freedom as a result of her father's illness. Her parents realized that their daughter needed more parental supervision.

Maybe you are feeling disturbed, isolated, or just stressed out. Your school counselor can help you get your priorities straight and eliminate nonessential activities. You will experience a great sense of relief when you devote your time and energy to things that really matter to you.

If you are experiencing inner turmoil, you need someone to talk to. If your school counselor is unable to help you, seek help from someone else. Friends are useful, but when you have very legitimate life problems you need someone older and wiser.

The logical place to start is with your parents, but they may be very busy, or you may not feel comfortable talking to them about personal issues. You need someone who can really listen and advise you. Who has been there for you in the past and has the knowledge and experience you need right now? It might be a relative, a neighbor, your minister, priest, or rabbi, a family friend, or even a favorite teacher. Or maybe someone else. (Perhaps talking to more than one understanding adult would give you a variety of ways to handle your problems.) You need to share your anger and conflicting emotions because unresolved inner turmoil can make you ill.

James is having problems dealing with his feelings and is not doing anything about it. He is angry for his mother who has MS and angry at the disease. "My emotions are so—well—the really bad ones are sort of bottled up and maybe they'll come out many years from now." Margo feels strongly that counseling is important for young people in your situation. Mary "highly recommends a support group." Jessy advises, "Get help. Talk to someone outside the family, outside the situation, whether it's a close friend or a support group or a psychotherapist." She sees a therapist regularly and finds it helpful. "I feel better talking to someone about my dad's MS."

You might try a support group for the teenagers of parents with MS. If one is available in your area, the MS Society can put you in touch with it. If you can't find your local chapter's telephone number, call 1 (800) 227-3166 in the United States or call 1 (800) 268-7582 in Canada and talk to someone. Perhaps with their help you can start a group. Support groups enable their members to focus on important issues that concern them. They give the participants a chance to vent their feelings and discuss specific problems in dealing with the disease. The leaders either have MS or know a lot about it. The group's focus is organized, and when members face a dilemma they get feedback or receive suggestions to improve their situation.

If an MS support group is not an option in your area, perhaps there's a group for the teenagers of adults who have chronic illnesses. Telephone the local chapter of the American Cancer Society or the American Heart Association and ask if there are meetings for people your age. If there are none, perhaps they have a suggestion.

Perhaps it would help to see a psychotherapist (a psychologist or psychiatrist) for a while. Men and women in these professions help people deal more effectively with their lives by listening to their problems and offering counsel. Psychiatrists are also medical doctors and thus are able to prescribe medication if necessary.

Psychotherapists are often very expensive, but some of them work on a sliding scale, adjusting the fee to what the client can afford. If your school counselor or family doctor is unable to help you find one, telephone the mental health department of your city or county government. You can also see a counselor at the master's degree level: an MA or MFCC (marriage, family, child counselor), a licensed clinical social worker (LCSW), or a master of social work (MSW). Some of these professionals are not available everywhere, so check your resources carefully. If you live near a medical school or university, there may be an outpatient mental health department where you can be treated at a reduced fee by a student under supervision.

Another thing you might try is physical exercise, the kind that gives you a real workout. Even if you're depressed and have no energy, a good workout can often give you renewed energy. Another remedy for occasional depression is this: When you're *not* feeling depressed, make a list of peaceful, pleasant activities that you enjoy, that make you feel good about yourself. Then the next time you feel depressed, do one of the things on your list. The pleasure won't last forever, but even brief relief is better than just being passively depressed. Depression and anxiety can have a severe effect on teenagers who feel isolated and unable to cope.

You're at a stage in your life where friends are your most meaningful contacts. They have begun to replace your parents and family as sources of important input in your life. Your friends affect the way you dress, your speech patterns, your walk, even such trivial things as whether you blow bubbles with your bubble gum or how you roll up your jeans. Most teenagers feel comfortable hanging out with their friends in groups. The activities of groups vary according to the teens' interests, but there is a clear connection between the kinds of things you do together and the depth of the friendships that you form. It is important that your outlook on life and the things that are significant to you be similar to those of your friends. The desire to be like others in your peer group may be stronger than your decisions as to what is correct behavior. You could wind up a very unhappy teenager in a lot of trouble if you do not select your friends carefully.

BREAKING THE LAW

Breaking the law is taking a chance and negatively affecting others by your actions. People who engage in such activities often don't believe in themselves and have difficulty relating to others. Sometimes they feel that those closest to them are not concerned about them.

You may be tempted to break the law as a way of

getting attention if your parents are preoccupied all the time. Perhaps you feel vulnerable if you're not dating anyone you like and relations with your friends are strained because of the family pressure you are under. School may be causing problems. If you are considering breaking the law to put a little excitement in your life, it's time to do some serious thinking. Why do illegal activities appeal to you? What do you hope to accomplish? What are your expectations? Lots of money? Prestige among your friends? Have you thought about the consequences of being caught? Being arrested, being sent to detention hall or perhaps prison are among the possibilities. Ask yourself if the benefits of breaking the law are worth the consequences.

Is there a choice for you? There always is. You can refuse to participate in illegal activities, which requires strength of will. You can avoid schoolmates who are a bad influence, perhaps by changing schools, or by working in your spare time. You could choose a responsible older person to confide in and call on if an illegal act seems like the only way out.

CHAPTER ◇ 4

Changes

The majority of people with MS are able to continue with their lives with only minor changes to accommodate occasional exacerbations. Even if someone does experience a change in walking status and requires an assistive device, he or she can still maintain an active life either at work or in the home. The children of these individuals do not suffer major changes in their life-styles, nor do they encounter many of the problems discussed in this book. The personal experiences related here are by teenagers whose parents are greatly affected by MS either mentally or physically, or both. Many of these parents participate in MS support groups, and their children were reached through those groups. Consequently, the personal experiences reflect families who have suffered a great deal. It must be stressed that people who suffer from severe MS are in the minority, and your parent may never experience the vast array of problems described.

Multiple sclerosis is often blamed when family members complain about the ill parent's increased moodiness, impatience, or recurring depression. In fact, the person's temperament may have been unsteady before the illness, and now MS is a convenient excuse. Also, teenagers are often critical of their parents and exaggerate their deficiencies; they may blame MS when it is their biased point of view that is at fault.

CHANGES IN YOUR PARENT'S BEHAVIOR

When your parent has been ill for a while, you may notice some behavioral differences that you're sure are new. You may be right. MS affects people in many ways, some quite obvious, others vaguer and more difficult to perceive. The demyelination that occurs can cause changes in the brain that could result in behavioral changes. You may notice your parent repeating himself or herself or having trouble coming up with an appropriate word. Perhaps your parent is occasionally euphoric (very high-spirited for no obvious reason) or sometimes does or says something you consider inappropriate. James was quite upset after reading his mother a poem he had written. As he neared the end, she turned the TV up loud and totally ignored him.

Other changes may make your parent more difficult to live with. James notices that his mother gets "huffy and puffy and acts like a kid. I get frustrated because we're not communicating properly, but I realize it's the MS that makes her act this way. She can't deal with any excitement at all; even good things freak her out. If I make her laugh too much or she's having too much fun, she'll get just as upset as if she's mad. She bursts out crying at anything. Lately I've noticed she's sometimes cruel and bitter and hardly has any sympathy or compassion. She doesn't care about how my days are any more. That really bothers me."

Jessy finds her father "irrational, moody, and depressed." Heather's mother is "very emotional and gets upset easily." Maria's father "has a short temper and little things get him aggravated, especially when he's not able to do things like other fathers."

Kevin's mother blamed everything on the MS and tried to make the family feel guilty because she had it. When they were planning to go out to dinner, she was never ready on time and would say, "It's taking me longer to get ready than you. Go without me. I'm sick." She would never go to new restaurants, only to familiar places. His mother sometimes got so upset and angry that she behaved irrationally. "I remember her losing her temper and running into us kids with her scooter."

David had a hard time dealing with the change in his mother's personality and emotional state. "It was difficult to be around her sometimes. She cried easily and would get angry over and over about the same things. It was really getting to me as she became more emotional about little things and turned them into a major problem. If she misplaced a pair of scissors, she would act like the world was coming to an end. She would be unreasonable and wouldn't talk rationally about it. I found it easier to avoid dealing with it at all. Then I went through a period of trying to discuss things with her. I said I'd talk to her about it only if she wouldn't cry and would be reasonable. If she began to get emotional, I'd just walk away. But I would always reassure her that I wasn't mad at her and was doing it for her own sake. This approach really helped. Now she's emotionally better and accepts that she can't do some of the things she used to."

Interestingly, problems that affect the mind often cause more distress than changes to the body. These difficulties can be influenced by sleep disruptions, tension, depression, stress, and fatigue, so they may change from day to day. Your parent may also experience other mental or emotional problems such as inability to concentrate, loss of organizational skills, rapid mood changes, poor short-term memory, and faulty problem-solving and decision-making.

Sean's father has memory problems that irritate Sean because they occur so frequently. "Dad blames a lot on the MS. I'm not exactly sure what is the MS and what isn't. It's recurring little things that he forgets—a phone message, locking my car after he drives it, or eating a meal I've prepared and left in the refrigerator when I'm rushing to work and don't have time to make something else. I'm sure he could overcome his forgetfulness if he made an effort. He just doesn't think things through. I remind him over and over about these things, but he still forgets and then says, 'I wasn't aware.' It happens all the time."

The need for constant reminders is really annoying, especially if you feel that your parent is making no attempt to improve. Try to be patient, and see if you can get your other parent to help. If your parent is having a memory problem, try getting an appointment/address book. Encourage your parent to write everything in it, such as appointments, people who must be phoned, chores to be done in the house, and the name, telephone number, address, and birthday and wedding anniversary dates of people close to him or her. Also available are tiny electronic organizers that fit into a pocket or purse and can record just about anything and replay it in an instant.

Perhaps your parent is using poor judgment and as a result making bad decisions. This can be really tough on you and the entire family. It is especially difficult if he or she is the parent who makes decisions for you. Maybe you are seeing situations in a more realistic way and feel that your parent does not realize all the ramifications of his or her decisions. The best thing you can do is to encourage your parent to do more research and to consult a trusted friend before finalizing a decision. If you believe your parent has shown poor judgment in making a decision, sit down together and go through all the steps that were taken to reach the conclusion. Tactfully point out errors you think were made along the way. If you make no headway, try to convince your parent that many experts say young people are better off if they make up their own minds and experience the consequences while they are still young. In that way they learn early how to make wise choices.

Many behavioral changes in people with MS result from the pressures of having the disease (plus other stresses that may be occurring in their lives), not from neurological damage. Dr. Stephen Rao, associate professor of neurology and psychiatry at the Medical College of Wisconsin, is quoted in "Let's Open Up the Subject of 'Personality Change'": ". . . 80 percent of the people who have MS and experience some psychological problem can cope and/or change and get on with their lives."[1]

Your parent may be experiencing physical difficulties as well as psychological ones, and you might be concerned that further physical disability will cause a similar increase in mental and emotional problems. Dr. Robert Heaton and his colleagues at the University of Colorado and Dr. William Beatty at the University of North Dakota have done a number of studies showing that there is only a

---

[1] Frames, Robin, "Let's Open Up the Subject of 'Personality Change'" in *Facts and Issues*, September 1989, reprinted from *INSIDE MS*, Winter 1988 (New York: National Multiple Sclerosis Society).

small relationship between psychological problems and physical limitations. They have also found that psychological problems are not usually affected by how long a person has had MS. Rather than getting worse as time goes by, your parent may even improve as he or she gets used to having MS and managing its symptoms.

If you and others in your household notice one or more of these changes in your parent with MS, these suggestions might help you:

1. Go with your parent to the neurologist to discuss the changes. The cause may be neurological, or it might be a psychological reaction to the trauma of having the disease.
2. Perhaps your parent needs to see a psychotherapist knowledgeable about MS. Discussing psychological symptoms may help to alleviate them. The therapist can help your parent develop a more positive outlook on life, which may ultimately ease some symptoms of the disease.
3. It may be helpful for your parent to join an MS support group or have a peer counselor, someone who also has MS, to talk to when necessary. People with MS can often be more understanding of each other's problems than others can be.
4. Do some research. Are there some courses or one-day seminars available that your parent can take to gain better coping skills?
5. Try to ensure that your parent does not ignore or deny having MS; that attitude can cause many problems. Help him or her remain as involved as possible in family activities, to avoid withdrawing from the world and becoming totally preoccupied with the disease. That does not mean that your

parent should go everywhere you go. It simply means that the family should include your parent in discussions of their activities and invite him or her to attend sporting events or school concerts or any other activities that involve them.

6. You and your family should be knowledgeable and compassionate about MS and the various problems associated with it. Your parent needs all your love and support.

Depression

Depression affects as much as thirty to forty percent of people who have MS at some point during the course of their illness. It is not known how much depression results from brain damage and how much from emotions about having the disease. It is the unpredictability of MS that is so difficult to deal with and so scary. Maybe your parent is grieving deeply for loss of physical or mental capacities. This grief often decreases as time passes, but some people have more trouble accepting their changing situation. Sometimes depression is caused by a feeling of loss of "self." Your parent may identify himself or herself as very sick and no longer a worthwhile human being. Margo noticed this problem and made sure she spent time every day with her mother, talking about her activities, her friends, and school. She also often told her mother how much she loved and needed her and how essential a part of her life she was.

Depression can have many different symptoms: inability to sleep, exhaustion, lethargy, crying for no apparent reason, irritability, and withdrawal. It is not necessarily the most severely disabled people who suffer from serious depression, but often those who lack the coping skills to deal with the changes and losses MS entails.

Your parent may express the depression as rage and resentment. Try not to take it personally if your parent is impatient with you, nor to let outward behavior confuse you. Chronic and severe depression can lead a person to feel that life is not worth living. But no matter how serious the depression, it can be treated by psychotherapy or medication, or both. It is important, however, to obtain treatment as soon as possible.

If treatment by a psychiatrist or psychologist does not relieve the depression, your parent can request a referral to a psychopharmacologist or a neuropsychologist. A psychopharmacologist is a specialist in medication protocols for psychiatric disorders. He or she may recommend special combinations of medications for patients who do not respond to those usually prescribed. A neuropsychologist can evaluate the depression for any organic contribution (e.g., brain cells that are not communicating properly) and recommend further medical evaluation and treatment accordingly. Either of these specialists can provide additional information about your parent's condition, including what you might expect in the future and what you may be able to do in the meantime.

MS is difficult for the whole family, but imagine what it must be like having to cope with the symptoms and stress of the disease, minute by minute, day by day? Following are some suggestions that a number of people with MS have found helpful in dealing with the disease. Some of the advice is from *Living with Multiple Sclerosis*.[2] Perhaps

---

[2] Wasserman, Lynn, with technical assistance, *Living with Multiple Sclerosis* (New York: National Multiple Sclerosis Society, 1978), pp. 14–15.

you can help your parent follow these recommendations:

1. "Take one day at a time." Deal with today's ups and downs; don't worry about tomorrow's.
2. Maintain a positive attitude. "Concentrate on your abilities rather than your disabilities."
3. "Keep as active as you can within the limits imposed by MS."
4. Modify your goals so they are realistic and attainable. Measure your achievements by what it is possible for you to do, not by what other people can achieve.
5. Change your values if necessary. Emphasize inner qualities rather than physical competence.
6. Plan your life so that you always have enjoyable events to look forward to.
7. Find an activity that gives you a sense of fulfillment and do it regularly: painting, volunteer work, collecting stamps, etc.
8. Keep your mind busy: Play games, do word puzzles.
9. Keep up your appearance. Being well groomed is important to your self-image.
10. Get lots of sleep and avoid fatigue.
11. Have numerous small meals rather than three large ones. Make sure there is always food in your stomach.
12. Exercise daily. It stimulates the circulation and improves digestion, elimination, and other bodily functions.
13. Communicate your thoughts and worries to people close to you, but don't dwell on them.
14. Do things for yourself when possible, but accept assistance when necessary.

You can help your parent make use of these suggestions. Encourage him or her to exercise regularly, and help if necessary. Think of things that will please your parent, that he or she can look forward to, and do them together. Bolster your parent's spirits. Jonathan has a sunshiny smile and a really "up" attitude to life. Just having him around the house makes his mother feel good. Play games together. Buy some crossword puzzle books that can help keep your parent's mind active. Make sure snacks are always within easy reach. Help your parent select clothes for the next day, and lay them out. Have soothing talks with your parent just before bedtime, to relax and help him or her sleep better. You'll probably think of lots of other things you can do to help your parent keep a positive, hopeful outlook.

Stress

In *Coping with Stress*,[3] stress is defined as the "body and mind's reaction to everyday tensions and pressures." Some of the signs of stress are "tiredness, . . . muscle tension, anxiety, indigestion, nervousness/trembling, sleeplessness . . . reduced or increased appetite, and grinding teeth/clenching jaws . . ."

Many studies have been conducted as to whether stress affects MS, but the results have been inconclusive. However, numerous experts and some doctors believe that there is a definite connection between stress and disease

---

[3] Adapted by The Development Team, Inc. from *Coping with Stress* © 1986, published by the National Multiple Sclerosis Society, New York. Used by permission of the Arthritis Foundation.

and that serious illness can result from inability to cope with strong stress. It is widely accepted that relaxation techniques can lessen stress and even help to heal a sick person. Stress can be alleviated in many ways; following are a few suggestions:

1. Yoga, involving breathing, stretching, and relaxation exercises, can be a wonderful tension releaser.

2. Psychotherapy can alleviate stress by enabling your parent to talk with an objective person. He or she may want to discuss MS, as well as other causes of stress, with someone other than family members.

3. Massage is a great reliever of stress. A forty-five-minute session daily or weekly would be of great benefit to your parent. Professional massage is quite expensive, but perhaps your family can afford one session and the masseur can show you or your other parent how to do it.

4. Meditation, besides being a spiritual connection with God, can be very relaxing, giving a sense of tranquility throughout the body and mind. You could find a book on meditation for your parent to use, or you could help him or her do the following meditation. You might even try it yourself.

This meditation should be done silently, at the same time and in the same place, early in the morning and at night, facing east if possible. The spine should always be straight and the eyes closed.

To begin, place the left thumb on the left nostril and breathe in through the right nostril to the silent count of 4. Close the right nostril with the index finger and don't breathe for the count of 16. Remove the thumb from the left nostril and breathe out to the count of 8. Repeat twice more. Then repeat with the opposite hand and opposite nostril three times.

Next do the neck exercises slowly, facing forward. Let the head fall forward three times, then backward three times; then to the right and left three times each, trying to reach the shoulders. Rotate the head to the right three times and to the left three times.

Next, recite any prayer you are comfortable with. The Lord's Prayer or Psalm 23 are suggestions.

Then say a healing prayer, addressed to God or to whomever you pray. Ask for what you desire and be specific about the healing you are requesting. Express gratitude for what you do have in life. Use your own language, speaking with respect.

Next say, "With Thy permission, Lord, I enter meditation." Sit silently for fifteen minutes the first time, gradually increasing to thirty minutes in later sessions. Focus on the word "God" or "Love" or "Healing" or any word that is spiritual to you. See the word imprinted on the inside of your forehead, between the eyebrows. Visualize the imprint as about the size of a thumbnail and on a small TV screen. That is hard to do, but even if you don't see the word, maintain the feeling for it. As you meditate more, you may see the image. When you are finished, offer thanks for the meditation in your own words.

Then repeat your healing prayer and end with any favorite prayer. Come out of the meditation gradually.

Your attitude throughout should be one of trust and expectancy. As you meditate more, you'll find your own style. Before the meditation, get into the mood and choose a special place that has good vibes. You can even burn white candles or incense to improve the vibes.

5. Visualization and affirmation have brought about wonderful changes in many people. To be effective, they must be done with a belief in the possibility of getting well.

To begin visualization, help your parent mentally to picture things he or she desires to do and would do if well. Your parent needs to experience the emotions associated with each activity as if actually doing it. While doing this, your parent should repeat affirmations, which are actually desires but are said as though already accomplished. Instead of saying, "I wish I could walk" or "I will walk," say "I am walking." The affirmations should be memorized so that they can be said with the eyes closed. The intensity and energy involved in saying affirmations should be so great that they are felt in the stomach.

Another kind of visualization is devising a scene that is particularly relaxing to your parent. To begin, your parent should concentrate on breathing slowly and evenly until tension is eased and a feeling of tranquility is achieved. While he or she sits with closed eyes, you can use a soothing voice and gentle words to create a vivid visual experience. Describe the scene in great detail so that it can be experienced by all your parent's senses. Talk about strengthening his or her immune system to overcome the multiple sclerosis. Have your parent see himself or herself as healthy again. Soothing music can have a positive effect on the visualization. At the end, have your parent use deep breathing again to come out of the visualization gradually, feeling alert yet peaceful. When you and your parent are comfortable with the procedure, you could make a tape recording of your voice for use when you are not available. Visualization is a way to share your love; you can both benefit from transforming that love into an experience that brings tranquility and hope.

CHANGES IN YOUR PARENTS' RELATIONSHIP

As we have discussed, your parent with MS may be suffering from emotional problems as a result of the disease. Some of these are caused by the stress of having such a serious and unpredictable illness; others may be the result of personality changes caused by the disease process. As a result, your parent may be short-tempered and verbally or physically abusive. Try to remember that your parent loves you as much as ever but is frustrated and perhaps does not have as much self-control as before.

Your parent may have become withdrawn and be too overcome with self-pity to relate to others. This may develop into a severe depression until your parent loses all energy and motivation and just sits staring blankly into space.

These emotional problems may create many difficulties for the whole family. You may find that both your parents are experiencing a great deal of anger. It may take time for them to realize that they are not angry at each other, but at the disease.

Your healthy parent will naturally feel burdened by all the extra work, and your parent with MS may try to help but be so slow as to do no good. Or your parent may insist on being independent and attempt impossible tasks, creating a mess that has to be cleaned up by your other parent.

Despite the physical burden, your healthy parent could probably handle the extra responsibility. But he or she may find it overwhelming to live with the unpredictability of multiple sclerosis as well as the changed behavior of your ill parent. Leslie remembers, "Mom had to do pretty much everything and really resented it when my

father insisted that things be done the way he wanted."
David says, "Mom had a need to continually remind
everyone that she has MS. When Dad came home from
work, she would complain about all the negative occur-
rences of the day. She took things out on him by constantly saying, 'I have MS and can't depend on anyone.'
Dad would push to do a lot for her, but he got worn
down by giving in to her. Finally, he couldn't stand her
emotional state any more. He had tried and tried, always
hoping she would be easier to get along with, but by the
time he left he had given up and wasn't willing to try
any more."

Sometimes the person with MS causes the breakup of
the marriage because it is too painful to have a healthy
mate serving as a constant reminder of all that he or she
used to do. Or your parent may just get tired of hearing
from others how giving and wonderful the healthy partner
is.

In addition to the emotional, mental, and physical
pressures your parents are undergoing, they may be having sexual problems as well. When MS is involved, sexual
desire may diminish on an emotional level because of
the many problems involved in living with the disease.
Or MS may cause physical difficulties that make sexual
activity awkward or impossible. Although there is no way
you can help with sexual problems, be aware that this
may be happening between them, adding to the many
hurdles they already face.

Not every family dealing with MS ends up in divorce.
Many stay intact and deal with the disease as just another
of life's challenges to overcome. Courtney's family has
experienced many financial and health difficulties (even
before MS), as well as problems with the children. But
throughout them all, "My parents have kept their sense of

humor and discuss anything that bothers them, and they each see the other's point of view. Their home is the center of their existence. Mom is pretty unstable when dealing with Dad's MS and is sometimes resentful and mean. But through it all my parents are loyal to each other and best friends. One of the reasons their marriage has lasted is that they both have a strong will to beat the odds."

Amber's father has had MS since before she was born. She says, "My family is not a typical one because my parents hardly ever argue. They're both dedicated to helping other people; they know it's the most important thing in life. They feel if they don't do it, no one else will." James's parents have been married a long time too. "Dad's a great person, and his inner strength has gotten him through Mom's MS, even though it's really been hard for him. We've discussed his attitude and he says, 'She's my wife, the person I fell in love with and married. I'm not going to toss her out because she's sick. Even if she gets worse, she's still my wife.'" When James's feelings are hurt by something his mother has said, his father comforts him, saying, "It's the disease. That's how it is." Lynn thinks her parents' marriage has lasted so long because, "My mom and dad believe that when you make a commitment you follow through with it and don't quit. My mom has a real commitment to life. That's what gets her through the difficult times with MS."

In "The Reality Behind the Perception," Pamela Cavallo mentions communication as "the most important element in the family dynamic . . ."[4] Unless people com-

---

[4] Cavallo, Pamela, MSW, CSW, "The Reality Behind the Perception" in *INSIDE MS*, Winter 1991 (New York: National Multiple Sclerosis Society), p.25.

municate effectively, no one knows what anyone else is thinking or feeling. Communication is extra important with the added tension created by MS and the various tasks falling on members of the family. You all need to share your differing opinions calmly and use open communication to solve your problems.

MS places great pressures on a marriage. You may be having a hard time watching the relationship between your parents change because of MS. Aside from suggesting counseling to them, helping out as much as possible, and causing as little stress as you can, there is not much you can do. But be aware that just as you didn't in any way cause the MS, you also didn't create the difficulties between your parents. They both love you and feel as responsible for you as they always did.

If your parents decide to divorce, do not choose to stay with your parent who has MS out of a sense of obligation or guilt or because you feel sorry for him or her. You need to be in a situation where your life continues with as few changes as possible. When Mickey's parents divorced, his mother moved out of the house even though she was the one with MS. She wanted her freedom, but she wanted her children to live in the house they grew up in and go to the same schools.

Whichever parent receives custody is supposed to ensure that you continue to have a place to live, food, schooling, and, of course, a lot of love. Whether you go to court and a judge makes the decision or your parents use a mediator to help them decide issues, you must be assertive in saying with whom you wish to live. Perhaps you should discuss some of the issues that directly involve you with an objective adult whom you trust. And remember, no matter with whom you live, you can have a close, loving relationship with your other parent. Many parents who divorce remain good friends, are supportive of each other, and share decisions related to their children.

CHANGES IN THE WAY YOU ARE TREATED

As a result of the upheaval in your home, one or both of your parents may knowingly or unknowingly be abusing you because of inability to cope with the stress of MS.

According to CHILDHELP USA, abuse that parents may inflict on their children is of four kinds.

1. Physical—when you are injured by a parent and it leaves marks, for example, burns, welts, or scars.
2. Neglect—when you or your siblings are neglected, are not supervised properly, or lack medical care.
3. Emotional—when you are spoken to in a way that might reduce your self-esteem; a parent saying, for example, "I wish you were never born" or "You've ruined my life" or "You always do everything wrong."
4. Sexual—when a parent (or anyone) approaches you in a sexual manner with or without your consent, or exposes himself to you, molests you, makes sexual remarks, or makes you watch a pornographic film.

Statistics show that one third of all girls and one fifth of boys are sexually abused before they reach age eighteen.

It might be helpful for you to know that parents who mistreat their children usually do not think well of themselves or may have a strong need to control other people. Sometimes they distrust people or organizations, and this isolation puts greater pressure on them. They may have experienced abuse when they were young, and it seems natural to them to continue the behavior with their own children. Or they may be having marital or communication problems within the family. If your father had physically abused your mother before she became ill, her illness may now make him feel angry and out of control, and he might displace his anger and violence on you. What might start simply as yelling at you may suddenly turn into loss of control and physical abuse. As you grow older and become more self-reliant, your parent may be unable to accept your new independence. A parent with low self-esteem might even feel intimidated by your increased size.

If you are being abused in any way, you must get help; otherwise the trauma will have long-lasting effects on you. Telephone the National Child Abuse Hotline at 1 (800) 422-4453, which operates 24 hours a day. Because of the large volume of calls, it may take a while before the phone is answered. A counselor will listen to your problems and discuss with you ways you can cope. Then you will be given the name of an agency in your area that can help you. You may be made part of a conference call so that the counselor at the Hotline can be sure that the local agency can provide the help that you need.

CHANGES IN WHERE YOU LIVE

Sooner or later, it will be time for you to move on, to explore the world, perhaps go away to college or have your own place. This is a difficult time for people who have a disabled parent; they are torn between what they want to do and what they feel they should do. Jessy feels trapped and resentful even though she lives on her own. Her father is in a wheelchair and looks forward to her weekly visits, but she would love to move to another state. She says, "I feel obligated to visit him, and I feel stuck in California." Heather is in a similar situation. She wants to move into an apartment of her own. "Mom wants me to continue living at home. And I don't know if it's because she has MS and wants my help or she just doesn't want me to grow up."

On the other hand, George's mother wants him to have his own life, and he plans to move to another state. They will keep in touch through weekly telephone calls. James was concerned for a long time because he wanted to transfer to a school across the country. Finally, "I discussed it with my parents, and to my surprise they said, 'Don't let us hold you back.'" Harris says, "Dad encouraged me to move out and not to let his condition hold me back. He wanted me to go on with my own life." David is very close to his mother, and although he wanted to move away from Los Angeles, he worried about how she would manage without him because his parents are divorced and she is in a wheelchair. She had told him he was the only one she could depend on, which made him feel very uncomfortable. "I felt a great weight on my shoulders. For a long time, what other people needed governed my choices. Finally I realized I had to put my own needs first or I wasn't going to be any good to anybody else." David has since moved far away, but he visits his mother occasionally and they often talk on the telephone.

When it was time for Lisa to go to college, she chose one very near home; but because she was a poor student, she needed to spend a lot of time studying. She was concerned about the almost constant care her mother needed. "I went to see the guidance counselor at college and told him of my dilemma. He suggested that I put a notice on the bulletin board for people wanting part-time work. Now I have three students who stay with Mom and take care of her at various times between classes. I'm relieved of the responsibility at those times, and she loves having lively young people around."

Part of caring for an ill parent is caring for yourself as well. Although you've been a real help at home, you have your own life to lead and should do so at the appropriate time with a clear conscience. It is often hard for parents to "let go" of their maturing children even if illness is not part of the situation. Because of your parent's special needs, your decision to leave may cause temporary anger and misunderstanding between you. If you can maintain a firm but sympathetic attitude, your parent will probably adjust to your decision and support your need for independence.

CHANGES IN YOUR FEELINGS

Throughout the changes that you and your family have been through and perhaps will continue to undergo, you may be feeling uncomfortable and somewhat embarrassed about the physical or emotional changes in your parent. Some of the teenagers interviewed for this book stopped bringing friends home for a time because of problems associated with the disease. Erica was one of them; she didn't bring anyone home for three years. "There was so much fighting in my house, and Mom would yell at me in front of my friends. Also, Mom was walking poorly, and I didn't want to answer questions about what was wrong with her." Kevin didn't bring friends home from the time he was thirteen. "My home was not a happy place. There was a lot of tension between my parents and lots of arguing. Mom would pick on me, and I didn't want my friends to say, 'Look at all the chores you have to do!'"

Heather and Maria also didn't bring anyone home for a couple of years. Heather was afraid that when her friends saw her mother's condition, "They would think I was different." Maria says, "Dad was always grumpy and irritable from the medication he was taking." And Shannon was embarrassed by her father's slurred speech.

Although some teenagers found it easier to deal with the situation by not inviting friends over, others appealed to their friends' compassion and maintained their previous life-style as much as possible. David said his mother was in a bad emotional state and got out of control over minor things. When he explained the situation to his friends, they understood and just ignored the disturbances she created. Lorene found her friends really helpful. "They would get stuff for Dad, like a drink or something." James says, "My friends would say hello to Mom and watch TV with her and tell her how they were doing. Everyone would enjoy each other, and it gave Mom a real lift to be with them." Some of Harris's friends understood his situation and others didn't. "Dad is the same as anyone else's dad, except he has an extra problem to deal with. I couldn't change my friends who were uncomfortable, and I couldn't change my situation. If I can't change something, I just accept it and go on. But as my friends were exposed more and more to my dad, they stopped being uncomfortable."

If you're embarrassed about the situation in your home, it's okay not to expose a new friend or a date to it right away. A long-term friendship, however, thrives on honesty and needs to incorporate all aspects of your life. You can explain to your friend what the situation is so that he or she knows what to expect. Chances are that your friend will be more accepting and understanding than you imagined. Heather stopped being self-conscious;

"I realized that Mom was a person. I invited friends over and discovered that one of them was a wonderful help; he cheerfully lifted Mom and carried her wherever she needed to go."

Your parent's situation may change, but until it does, you'll have to live with it, so try to make the best of your predicament. Instead of concentrating on your parent's negative qualities or appearance, make a conscious effort to focus on the good traits and abilities that still exist. Sean now appreciates, from watching his father, "how hard it is to have a serious illness and see your body deteriorate. I feel it's important to make the most of a bad situation." Mickey says, "In dealing with a parent who has a disabling disease, it can either be a negative or a positive experience. It's up to you."

CHANGES IN YOU

One of the by-products of living with a serious disease like multiple sclerosis are the qualities you'll develop in your own character—fine qualities that will always be with you, making you a stronger and better human being and attracting people to you throughout your life.

These qualities will not come easily. They will develop through years of worry and caring and having to do things you don't want to do. They'll come so slowly that you won't even sense their arrival, but they will come. It may help you to read the following stories of other teenagers who have a parent with MS; they describe their home situation and discuss how they've grown stronger and more resilient as a result of their experiences.

When Heather was nine years old, her mother was diagnosed with MS. Heather felt helpless and out of control and very angry. "I resented the MS and wondered,

'Why us? There's bad people in the world; why pick on the good ones?'" Many responsibilities fell on Heather's shoulders. "I became the mom, and that sometimes made me angry. I had to grow up fast. I had to get dinner for everyone and get my younger brother and sister to school. I also kept the house neat. My mom is a fussy housekeeper and would get upset if there were any crumbs on the floor. I tried to do things before Mom saw them." Although Heather was busy with chores at home, she still found time for friends and other activities. She has developed into a person very concerned with accessibility for the disabled. "I notice if buildings and malls are accessible to wheelchairs. And I'm more out-spoken. If I see someone parking in front of a ramp, I ask them to park elsewhere. I really want to help people more than I used to, especially those who are different."

Joe says, "I've always respected my father and have shaped my life like his: to be as honest as possible, a good citizen, and a good human being. I've tried to make him proud of me." From his exposure to MS, Joe says, "I am more sensitive to people's needs, and I tell them I love them when it's appropriate. I'm more aware and compassionate than I used to be, especially with the disabled. I have a sense of reality about being disabled in life and the possibility of its happening to anyone. I'm going to be an architect and design buildings with the disabled in mind."

Courtney's father was diagnosed with MS just a few years ago, and already she has made some changes in her life. "I use great patience to deal with someone with a disability. I've become very compassionate, and I've chosen a profession that enables me to work with very ill patients in the hospital."

James's mother has had MS for many years, and he and

his father take care of her, along with an attendant. James is very angry about the MS. "It's so frustrating—like watching someone trapped. I wish I could do something. I've been dealing with it so long that I'm used to it by now. But it seems so long since Mom was totally functional. It's like the family's not balanced, like not having a mother in some ways. I really try—I feel like she's still my mom and I include her in my life as much as possible." About the effects the disease has had on him, James says, "It has intensified and made stronger the qualities I've always had. I'm more patient and understanding and compassionate. I'm also more cynical than I used to be, because I realize life is not fair. When I was a kid and something was unpleasant, I went to sleep at night and hoped it would be gone by morning. Now I know some things don't go away—you have to face them head-on and deal with them."

When Mary was thirteen years old, her mother was diagnosed with MS. They live in a single-parent home with Mary's brother. It has been hard for Mary, because she always had lots of chores to do as well as her schoolwork and helping her mother. But she has developed some fine qualities in the process. "I have a sensitivity for people and the things they may have to deal with. I'm more compassionate than I used to be, and I have a willingness to find out about people and not be stopped by a disability."

Harris's father was diagnosed with MS before Harris was born. Harris found his early teens very difficult. "I was trying to grow up within my own age and was forced to accept a lot of responsibility. I matured faster than my friends and always felt a little older. As a result, I didn't hang around with kids my own age. I joined a youth organization and met older kids who became my friends.

Because I was maturing so fast, I demanded a lot of freedom from my parents. When I was in high school I got into pot and drank and sometimes stayed out all night with girls. I made some mistakes, but I learned from them." Since his father was unable to do many things, Harris gained experience in repairing cars, appliances, and lawn mowers. He worked in the yard, weeding, mowing the grass, planting, watering, and helping cut down trees. He also helped his mother in the house. You might think he'd grow up bitter and angry from all this responsibility, but he didn't. He says, "I would do just about anything for a friend or even a stranger. I'm compassionate and sensitive to those who are physically and mentally challenged. I always offer help to people having trouble walking."

Leslie remembers her father always playing ball with her when she was a little girl. Now he can't, and she really misses that, but listening to music and reading books enables them to spend peaceful time together. This has strengthened their relationship. Not having a father to do physical things for her really changed her. "I learned how to fix cars and change the oil, which I wouldn't have learned if Dad had done it. I also came out a lot tougher than if I had had a father to protect me."

Kevin was eight years old when his mother was diagnosed with MS, and he feels he was cheated out of a real mother. "I felt all alone at home; there was no one to talk to. My brother was away at school. Even when he was home, we weren't close because we're different from each other. We didn't stick together to help each other. Now my brother and I relate better, but we live far apart and rarely see each other. I felt cheated out of a childhood, and I really resented all the chores I had to do— helping Mom in and out of her van and transferring her from a chair to her scooter and on and off the toilet, besides chores in the house. I had the responsibilities of an adult, but not the freedom. I've had a dramatic, traumatic life." And yet Kevin has benefited from his early maturity; it has resulted in a strong inner drive to achieve that has enabled him to excel at school and extracurricular activities. Kevin has also developed a lot of admirable qualities: "I'm open-minded, tolerant, selfless, realistic (but a bit of a pessimist), sensitive, and romantic."

Erica says, "I find it hard to accept the fact that I can't do some of the things with my mom like other kids can— going horseback riding or shopping at the mall or roller skating." But they still have fun together. "We buy fabric and make clothes, go to movies, watch videos at home, and play cards." For a time after the diagnosis, Erica was really angry at God. "Why my mom?" she asked. With divorced parents, she felt all alone. "I don't have a father to turn to when I need help. I used to relate to my older brother, but he tried to molest me two years ago so we're not close any more. But all this has brought me really close to Mom. I learned when I was very young to help in the house—emptying the dishwasher, mopping the floor, grocery shopping, and weeding in the yard." Erica is very loyal to her mother. "She took care of me when she could; now I'll take care of her when she needs it." Erica is aware that a disabling illness can strike anyone at any time, so she lives life fully. "I'm involved in lots of activities. I want to do it all now."

Royal's father sometimes has to take drugs for his MS. "It's hard to deal with. He's so out of it—spaced out. About once a year he has a bad exacerbation. He has a decrease in his muscle control and is confused and less lucid. I help by moving him around and lifting him in and out of his wheelchair. It's a bummer that this happened to him. Dad has a pretty good outlook on life; I admire that and talk to him a lot to try to keep his spirits up. Living with his MS has put the importance of life into perspective for me—we're not immortal, and perfect health is not guaranteed. I really appreciate my own mobility and don't take it for granted."

Jonathan was fourteen years old when his mother told him she had MS. He didn't know anything about the disease and refused to read about it: "I didn't want to face it." But he did have to deal with it as his mother became more disabled. He felt "hurt, helpless, and angry at the MS." He had to help at home. "I did the dishes and all the grocery shopping and all-around helping out. I was angry at the way things were. At first I was embarrassed when Mom started using a cane, but as I got older I didn't care what other people thought. I became more understanding of what disabled people go through. I do my best to be a loving son to Mom and to understand her problems. I appreciate my health and don't take it for granted."

Maria is very sad when she thinks of how MS has changed her father, who used to be very active. He doesn't like talking about his illness, but she watches him carefully. "I can tell when the MS is not going well. I won't ask him if it's the MS, but I help him out at those times, like going to the store with him. I used to be upset if Dad wasn't feeling well and couldn't take me places. Now I realize it's the disease. I'm disappointed, but not mad like before. I'm more compassionate and under-standing than I used to be."

Stuart felt "sad and concerned" when his mother told him her diagnosis. He was confused and shocked, and he detached himself emotionally. That way he found it easier to deal with the situation. He is less detached now, and even though he no longer lives at home, he lends a hand whenever he can. His attitude to disabled people has changed. "Before, I saw disabled people as different; now I realize they're the same as me. I get really annoyed when I see a healthy person park in a disabled space, and I always feel obligated to say something about it."

Sean's father was diagnosed with MS before Sean was born. Sean has gained much inner strength and has a great deal of admiration for his father from watching him deal with MS. "I'm a more positive person now when it comes to handling adverse situations."

Jessy says, "I have a hard time dealing with my anger. It's awful watching someone you love deteriorate before your eyes. But still, I sometimes get upset at Dad, at how helpless he is. I have to cut his meat for him, and he's fatigued at the end of the day. But I've realized it doesn't help the situation to be upset. The MS has forced me to deal with my father. Before I could just blow him off. Now we relate better."

David was eleven years old when his mother was diagnosed with MS. As he grew up, there was a lot for him to do at home. "I helped her get into bed and onto the toilet, drove her places, went shopping with her, and also washed the dishes. It was tough. I tried not to treat her any differently because of her illness, even though she was sometimes very unreasonable. When I felt I was close to my breaking point, I got out of the house. I had a few close friends to whom I talked about what was going on and unloaded my feelings. They were understanding and helped. I got much stronger and realized what my priorities are. Now I can make good decisions for myself."

Although Thomas's father goes to the Rehab Center at the hospital every morning to work out, the rest of the time he is at home and Thomas has total responsibility for him. "He needs twenty-four-hour care, and he's always there. Sometimes I want a break. I help him get into the shower so he doesn't fall, get his food for him, do the grocery shopping, and keep everything so he can get to it. I'm concerned about his health because he has such a terrible diet, but he refuses to change it." Before Thomas's dad got MS he was very violent, and Thomas stayed out of the house as much as possible. Now he is too sick to get violent. "Sometimes Dad still gets out of hand, but I know it doesn't do any good to get angry. I really don't want to live with him; I do it out of a sense of responsibility. I've learned it's important to think of and help other people. I respect life and feel lucky that I don't have something like MS. And I've developed patience and more patience."

Shannon finds that she can deal better with everyday problems than she used to. "Little problems don't seem as big anymore, like when I have fights at school with my friends. I'm more understanding of the problems people have. And I appreciate whatever Dad can do. I listen more to what he says and try to be agreeable."

Frank has never been embarrassed about his father's disability. On the contrary, he's always been very proud of him. "When he first started to use a wheelchair, I felt a bit uncomfortable, but now I'm used to it and it doesn't bother me at all. It's hard for me to deal with the fact that he can't do things he used to do. And I know that even if he has promised to be somewhere, if it's hot he won't show up. That's okay. I'm used to it. We treat each other exactly the way we always did. Because I look out for Dad, I've become a more helpful person generally. I have more respect for handicapped people and understand what they're going through."

Kathleen is a typical teenager, and her moodiness is a common characteristic of her age. She realizes how much she loves her parents. "I'm concerned about not upsetting my dad, so I'm careful not to argue with him. And I don't take my bad moods out on my parents." Kathleen has observed some changes since the diagnosis four years ago. "We're much closer as a family and really care about what's going on with each other. And I've also noticed that I'm a more caring person."

All these young people would love to change the fact that their parent has MS. Some of them have adjusted well to the situation; others are unhappy in their home life and would like to move out. But they all are making the best of it for now, because they know they are loved and needed and they feel a sense of responsibility to return some of the care that their parents gave to them when they were able to.

The giving and sharing and hard work these teenagers are experiencing are developing them into mature, responsible young adults, well equipped to deal with the ups and downs of life. As a result, they will be better friends, marriage partners, parents, and employees.

CHAPTER 5

Helping Your Parent

ATTITUDE IS CRUCIAL

After the diagnosis of MS is made, family members are often very concerned about the health and comfort of the person who is not well. This concern often causes them to ignore their own needs, and soon everyone may feel frustrated and bitter. Not only will you begin to feel overwhelmed by seemingly endless responsibilities, but your parent also will suffer, mentally and physically, from being so dependent. Your parent must learn to function independently up to his or her capabilities. You must learn to strike a balance between helping when you're needed and encouraging as much self-reliance as possible.

Your attitude is all-important here; it is as crucial as the help you give. If you focus on your parent's weaknesses, you will be overwhelmed by negative emotions. But if you care for your parent in a helpful, nonjudgmental manner, you will have a positive influence on the rest of your family. As your parent's condition fluctuates, try not to dwell on the past but encourage as much effort as possible from your parent.

THE IMPORTANCE OF NUTRITION

If one of your chores is shopping for groceries or preparing meals, you should consider nutrition for your parent with MS (and for the rest of the family as well). It is common sense that proper food leads to good health and energy. You need lots of energy for all your activities, and your parent who has MS needs to stay as healthy as possible to fight infection and fatigue.

You can get suggestions for serving nourishing food from the MS Society or by calling the Federal Information Center at 1 (800) 726-4995. In Canada call your local Public Health Clinic.

According to the National Multiple Sclerosis Society, no specific diet has been scientifically proven to alleviate the symptoms or arrest the progression of MS. However, some experts believe that certain diets are helpful.

Roy Laver Swank, M.D., Ph.D., and Barbara Brewer Dugan are the authors of *The Multiple Sclerosis Diet Book*. Dr. Swank believes that his low-fat diet, when followed conscientiously, reduces the frequency and severity of exacerbations in MS patients and causes the disease to progress more slowly. Many people in the medical profession believe that his diet has not been adequately tested in controlled scientific studies and disagree with the book's philosophy. However, some doctors consider it an excellent diet to follow for general good health.

Robert W. Soll, M.D., Ph.D., and Penelope B. Grenoble, Ph.D., are the authors of *MS: Something* Can

Be Done and You *Can Do It.* They believe in doing everything possible to avoid infection (and treat it promptly if it occurs) and that it is important to identify foods that bring about disagreeable symptoms and worsen MS. They use a step-by-step process to help patients find out what foods they are allergic to and to develop a new diet using only natural foods.

Your library may have these as well as other books on diets for people with MS. If they are unavailable, your library can probably borrow them from another library. After you have read a few nutrition books, discuss them with your family so that the type of diet you all follow will be based on a group decision.

Once you are known as the food shopper or preparer for your family, you will be deluged with unsolicited advice. Be open to suggestions, but always consult with your family before making major dietary changes.

Food shopping and preparation can be both challenging and rewarding. When marketing, use a list to avoid forgetting items, and always look for specials to help the family budget. Even though you are following a diet, preparing food can be a creative experience. Mark is careful not to overcook vegetables, knowing that too much heat destroys their nutritional value. He also takes time to arrange the food as attractively as possible to encourage his father to eat. Get some easy-to-follow cookbooks, and you'll be surprised how much fun it is to try new recipes.

PHYSICAL THERAPY AND EXERCISE

Many people with multiple sclerosis derive great benefit from physical therapy. A therapist can design an exercise program specifically for your parent's needs. If you take an interest in the therapy sessions, you can learn how to perform the exercises properly and can help your parent do them at home. You can make a chart to keep track of progress and encourage him or her to follow the therapist's instructions. It is important to do the exercises regularly; the therapist will probably recommend three times a week. Your parent may need encouragement; you can help by keeping count or by providing company while the exercises are being done.

Erica paid careful attention when the physical therapist showed her how to help her mother exercise, and she helped at home by rotating and massaging her mother's feet. Erica also held her waist to steady her while she walked sidewise to strengthen her legs. They did this every night. When they started, her mother was having great difficulty in walking and was using Canadian crutches. The doctor said if her condition got any worse, she would need a wheelchair. But perseverance succeeded. After a time Erica's mother walked with only one crutch, and later just a cane. Now she uses no aids at all. It took eight years of hard work, but they're both very proud of their accomplishment.

The physical therapist will suggest stretching and strengthening exercises to help your parent function as fully as possible. People with MS have to remember to stop exercising before they get tired and to rest as needed afterward. Whether a person is ambulatory or in a wheelchair, a well-designed exercise program can be beneficial.

The therapist can help improve your parent's sitting and standing posture to decrease stress on muscles and joints. The therapist can also suggest the best positioning in bed to reduce muscle stiffness and help your parent sleep more comfortably.

If your parent has difficulty walking, the physical therapist might suggest an assistive device such as a cane, walker, brace, or crutches. Sometimes one may be needed temporarily during an exacerbation. If your parent has not needed one before, he or she may resist the idea. Often an outsider such as a therapist can persuade him or her of the value of a walking aid. If your parent complains that a walking aid makes him or her feel dependent, you can explain that the opposite is actually true. If a person needs an assistive device and does not use one, he or she is unsafe and completely dependent on other people.

A physical therapist is also trained to give massage, which has a wonderfully soothing effect on anyone with a physical problem. If massage is indicated, the therapist will teach you how to do it correctly. If your parent's legs tend to become stiff, massage may temporarily loosen the muscles, making walking easier. Another benefit of massage is that it gives you and your parent a peaceful, loving experience to share. If there are conflicts in the house, you may find that the relaxation you provide will help ease some of the strains.

Your parent may decide not to see a physical therapist, but to do exercises independently. Swimming is the best type of exercise, because it requires the use of so many muscles. The water temperature is very important; if it is too hot, it will exhaust your parent. Some pools offer exercise classes in the water.

Yoga is a wonderful form of exercise that can be modified to benefit many levels of disability. It can have a positive effect on posture, balance, flexibility, endurance, and mobility. The MS Society sometimes sponsors yoga classes designed to help people with MS with the physical problems the disease entails.

Another activity that you and your parent can do together is tai chi. Tai chi increases energy without strain-

ing the body. Since the emphasis is on individual progress, modified exercises can be done by weak or even
wheelchair-bound people. It is a great experience to
share with your parent. Your input, encouragement, and
participation can have a positive effect on both of you.
You're an asset to the get-well team; don't ever forget it!

Walking Difficulties

If your parent has trouble walking, movement in a pool
can be very beneficial. Dr. Randall Schapiro, director of
the Fairview MS Center in Minneapolis and clinical
professor of neurology at the University of Minnesota,
advocates beginning walking exercises in a pool, where
movement requires less effort than on land. You can go
into the pool with your parent and help with movement
and balance activities. You could also bring a portable
tape player with your parent's favorite music to make the
procedure more pleasant.

You can also help your parent do two exercises that
simulate walking, utilized by the A.R.E. Clinic in
Phoenix, Arizona. It is important always to remember
that any movement that causes pain should be stopped
immediately. Have your parent lie face down on the bed
with legs straight and arms beside the hips. You should
kneel at the foot of the bed. Have your parent raise the
right arm so that it is straight out at the shoulder and bent
to 90° (a right angle) at the elbow (or as close to that as
possible). At the same time, he or she should move the
right leg so it is straight out at the hip and bent to a 90°
angle at the knee (or as close to that as possible). If your
parent cannot do this alone, you can help by gently but
firmly moving the arm or foot into the correct position.
Return to the starting position and repeat the movement

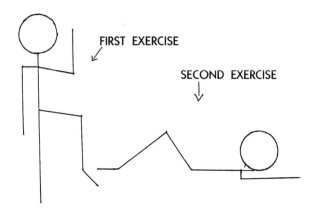

FIRST EXERCISE

SECOND EXERCISE

on the other side. Your parent's body should be angled slightly toward the side that is moving and face that side also, looking at the hand that is up.

The second exercise is done lying on the back. Your parent should bend the right knee to a right angle to the body (or as close to that as possible), at the same time swinging the left arm up and back as far as possible without pain. Repeat with the left leg and right arm. If your help is required, encourage yourr parent to do as much as possible while you gently assist the movements.

With both of these exercises, movement of the right leg plus the left one constitutes a count of one. Start slowly with one or two repetitions and gradually work up to twenty. The most important thing is for your parent to achieve a smooth motion and move the arms and legs at the same time.

As with anything new, your parent should check with the doctor or physical therapist before starting these exercises.

Stairs are likely to be very difficult for your parent if walking is a problem. Have your parent use the stronger leg first to go up and the weaker leg first when going down. There is a saying for this: "Up with the good, down with the bad." Joe's father is in stable condition but needs help on stairs. Joe cautiously stays behind him when going upstairs and in front of him when going down, in case he should slip.

If stairs at your front door are a problem for your parent, it may be time to put in a ramp. The MS Society can give you names of companies in your area that build ramps. Lee's father has an immobile left side that makes moving about very difficult for him. Lee has had carpentry training, and he and his brother built a wooden ramp at their front door. It is about 11 feet long and goes over the step. It took them just one day to build, and their father appreciates their efforts every time he uses it.

Walking is something that healthy people take for granted, but for someone with MS it can be a true ordeal. Every single step is a tremendous physical effort. If balance is a problem, walking demands total concentration. Be patient and loving with your parent even though you may be embarrassed or upset by the way he or she walks. Despite MS, your parent loves you and needs your patience and tolerance now more than ever.

Special Difficulties

If your parent is bedridden, the strain on your family will be great, and it is important to get help. Your local MS chapter may have a respite program that provides temporary help to enable the primary caregiver in your home to have some free time. Lacking that, they will be able to give you names of agencies that offer temporary or permanent help. If your family can afford it, a full-time attendant would relieve a great deal of stress.

This is a good time to sit down as a family group and

have a brainstorming session to think of all the people who might help. Think of everyone you know who could relieve you, even if only for a few hours—relatives, friends, neighbors. Also consider the parents of your good friends. You will find that many people you know are kind and caring and will extend themselves to help you. Don't hesitate to ask someone who always seems busy. Frequently, the busiest people are so well organized that they are the best able to fit something extra into their schedule.

A schedule should be arranged in your home, written down and posted for everyone to see. Most important of all, the schedule and your family must be flexible. Unexpected situations arise when one of you won't be able to be there, and the rest of the family must be pre- pared to pitch in. Reevaluate the assignments fairly regularly so that chores can be traded according to pref- erence. While you're scheduling time to help your parent, be sure to schedule each member's time too; it's important that you all have lives of your own outside of your home responsibilities.

Regardless of individual chores, each person in your family needs to be familiar with the entire routine of care for your parent, in case a last-minute substitution must be made. You should all know how to read a thermometer, give a bed bath, insert a catheter, dress and undress your parent, and move him or her from the bed to the wheel- chair and back again. If your parent cannot turn over at night, someone will have to move him or her every two or three hours to avoid pressure sores. Pressure sores occur where a bone is close to the surface of the skin. Pressure exerted on that spot decreases circulation, causing the tissue to break down and sores to develop. Pressure sores are very difficult to heal and can be a source of infection.

But they can be prevented. Check your parent's skin every day and watch for unusually pale or red areas. Gently rub lotion there, using a circular motion. Relieve the pressure in that area by changing your parent's position every few hours or by placing a pillow under the spot.

Although multiple sclerosis is not a terminal disease, complications can arise in the later stages of the illness. This is most common when a person spends most of the time in bed or in a wheelchair. These complications, if not recognized and promptly treated, can be life-threatening. The most common complications are recurrent infections that start in the urinary tract and spread throughout the body; lower respiratory problems such as pneumonia, and severe pressure sores. In practically every instance, these and other complications can be prevented or treated by keeping your parent as healthy as possible, having good nursing care, and calling the doctor immediately if a change in condition occurs. Early intervention is essential. To help your parent avoid infection, limit your own exposure to persons who have colds or the flu.

HELPING YOUR PARENT BECOME MORE INDEPENDENT

Occupational therapy can be of great benefit to people who are disabled. This is the topic of "Occupational Therapy Is Important . . . when you are diagnosed with multiple sclerosis." Some aspects of being self-sufficient are: "Managing fatigue through learning to conserve energy, simplify work and deal with stress; making the most of available body strength and coordination; providing tools and techniques to promote independence in the home, including modifying the environment and compensating for difficulties in thinking and planning, visual problems and loss of sensation."[1] OT also helps with vocational guidance and training.

Occupational therapists can be found in home-health agencies, hospitals, and private practice. Your parent's doctor can probably give you a referral.

The therapist may suggest some aids to help your parent function more independently. Many aids can be purchased from medical supply companies without seeing an occupational therapist. Among them are: built-up eating utensils that are easier to hold than regular ones, "reachers" to pick up objects on the floor, and aids for dressing and undressing. In the bathroom, your parent might need grab bars to help with getting on and off the toilet. A commode can be moved to the bedside for convenience; some have adjustable legs to fit over the toilet and function as a raised toilet seat. A plastic chair for the shower is considered a necessity by many people. A hand-held showerhead is very helpful; some even have a button to turn off the water flow. There are also devices to help a disabled person get in and out of the bathtub. All these products vary in cost. Check with the various places listed under "Medical Equipment and Supplies" or "Hardware-Retail" in the Yellow Pages of your telephone book, or consult your local chapter of the MS Society.

Now is a good time for you to take a critical look through your house and see what can be done to make it easier for your parent to get around. There should be wide open areas uncluttered by plants, knickknacks, or

---

[1] Developed by Frankel, Debra, "Occupational Therapy Is Important . . . when you are diagnosed with multiple sclerosis," adapted from an American Occupational Therapy Association publication (New York: National Multiple Sclerosis Society, 1990).

unnecessary furniture. Your parent may get tired walking, so be sure chairs are handy throughout the house. Remove any scatter rugs to prevent tripping, and look for other obstacles that might hinder your parent's self-sufficiency. Try to anticipate situations before they occur, so that your home is a safe place in which your parent can maintain maximum independence.

DIFFICULTIES WITH SPEECH

Although people with MS seldom have severe speech problems, it is not uncommon for someone to experience difficulties with speech at some time during the course of the disease. In "You Deserve Freedom of Speech,"[2] Dr. Kathleen R. Helfrich-Miller, Ph.D., CCC, a speech-language pathologist, states that such speech defects may result from "poor coordination or weakness of muscles in the tongue, lips, or palate. The symptoms may include: slurred speech, vocal harshness, lowered volume, change in tone and speech rhythm, inappropriate stress, and a reduced rate of speaking." She continues, "For people with MS, the severity of the problems and the ease of correcting them depend on the extent of neurological damage." No matter what the symptoms, however, speech can almost always be improved.

If your parent is having speech problems, suggest first that he or she speak more slowly. When people with speech problems talk fast it is more difficult to understand them.

No one's speech damage is exactly like anyone else's. Each person functions at a different level and has to work

[2] Frames, Robin, "You Deserve Freedom of Speech" in *INSIDE MS*, Spring 1991 (New York: National Multiple Sclerosis Society), p.28.

accordingly to correct speech difficulties. For mild cases of speech disorder, Dr. Helfrich-Miller advises that "often simple exercises and improved posture can help." Your parent must do speech exercises independently but might need encouragement and moral support from you. You can help plan a schedule for the exercises to make sure they are done. You might also set up a mirror so your parent can see whether they are being done correctly.

If speech therapy and exercises seem not to help, various devices are available to aid in communication. The National Multiple Sclerosis Society in New York can provide information about them. With a prescription from a doctor, some health insurance companies will pay a percentage of the cost.

James's mother began doing exercises to improve speech problems. James recalls, "The exercises helped while she did them, but then she got lazy and stopped doing them. She can still speak but just won't make the effort." She talks in a whisper so low that no one can hear. So James and his father made a letter board for her. Shaped like a large picture frame, it has a metal piece at the back to hold it at a 45° angle. On the front are four rows of plastic letters placed in alphabetical order. James's mother points at the letters to spell out the words she wants, and James or his father says them out loud. The system works very well for them, and James got to spend some quality time with his father while they made the letter board.

ASSISTANCE DOGS

If your parent with MS has a lot of trouble seeing and walking and is alone all day or has to walk to work, perhaps an assistance dog would be helpful. Assistance dogs are trained to do many things such as assisting a person up and down stairs, carrying items, picking up a telephone, retrieving items that have been dropped, and helping a person cross streets. The problem with an assistance dog is its care. If your family gets one, perhaps your contribution could be feeding, walking, and bathing it; and you might welcome the relationship.

The National Multiple Sclerosis Society in New York has a list of places that train assistance dogs. If your family is considering purchasing one, you should read the article "Cindy and Murphy" by Susan Price, published in *INSIDE MS*, Winter 1991.

INVISIBLE MS

We have discussed how physical therapy and occupational therapy can make life easier for your parent with MS. However, a large group of people with multiple sclerosis have different problems. They may suffer from fatigue, bladder or eye problems, or pain, symptoms that cannot be observed by you or anyone. Suffering from invisible MS, they are just as ill as anyone who is physically disabled. Maria's father had many symptoms when he was diagnosed with MS. His vision was blurry, he was always tired, and he had constant numbness and tingling throughout his body. With treatment, his vision is back to normal and he has regained over eighty percent of the feeling in his body, but he still has symptoms of invisible MS.

Fatigue

Some people with MS only suffer from fatigue, and they are often mistakenly called lazy. Their fatigue can be caused by a variety of things: high temperatures (the weather or a hot bath), stress, a large meal, strenuous physical activity, an infection, or fever. Many people find that their symptoms are worse in hot or humid weather. If your summers are hot, try to obtain a window air conditioner for the room where your parent spends most of the time. (It may be tax-deductible, so keep the receipt). If that is impossible, keep the drapes and blinds closed against the heat of the sun. Monica helped plan her mother's days so that the most strenuous tasks were done when it was coolest. Monica also had a real brainstorm. "I bought Mom a pair of real thin cotton socks. I soaked them in cold water and put them on her feet wet. As they dried, they really helped keep her cool."

Dr. Robert M. Herndon, director of the Center for Brain Research and the MS Clinic at the University of Rochester, New York, says that people with MS may suffer from fatigue for the following reasons:

1. Nerve fibers that are demyelinated utilize more energy than healthy fibers when transmitting nerve impulses. Fatigue of these nerve fibers results in a lack of strength and coordination in the body.
2. The restrictions and upset of having MS can lead to fatigue.
3. Additional effort is needed by the healthy muscles when other muscles are not strong. The strong muscles naturally tire faster if they are overworked.
4. Everyone experiences some muscle fatigue after doing a task, but it happens faster in those with MS.

You may have noticed that your parent tires much faster than previously and takes longer to recover. He or she may start a task and keep going energetically for quite a while, then suddenly run out of steam. Dr. Floyd Davis, director of the MS Center at Rush-Presbyterian-St. Luke's Medical Center in Chicago, says that a person need not work long and hard to get tired. Exhaustion may follow a nonstrenuous task done for only a short time. Merely writing a letter or reading can be tiring to a person who has problems with fatigue.

As a result of fatigue, a person may experience sluggish muscles, trembling, weakness, tingling or numbness in various parts of the body, or difficulties with speech or vision. There may also be decreased tolerance toward others and loss of enthusiasm for things that were previously important. Occasionally the fatigue gets so intense that new symptoms may appear or previous symptoms recur. Bed rest for several days is recommended as a remedy. If that is not effective, the doctor should be informed. It is important for the person to get enough sleep at night and to nap during the day as necessary.

Fatigue is sometimes confused with depression. If it is really fatigue, the sluggishness disappears; if it is depression, the person remains apathetic. Sometimes severe fatigue causes depression; in such case, drugs may be helpful.

The body varies in temperature throughout a 24-hour cycle. It is lowest at 2 to 3 a.m. and highest between 3 and 6 p.m. When the body temperature is high, people with MS feel more fatigued and are unable to do as much as usual. This is likely to be around dinner time, so if your parent with MS is the meal preparer, you or your siblings should help out by setting the table, clearing it after dinner, and washing the dishes.

You can also help by being alert to when your parent seems to have reached his or her physical limit. George looks out for his mother. "I always know when Mom's exhausted because she gets so crabby. I remind her that she's tired and tell her to go to bed for a while." Rests should be taken before doing a vigorous task, possibly during it, and afterward. Tiring things should be done early in the day when energy is at its peak, but even then your parent should not push to the point of exhaustion. Joe says, "We schedule social events we do together around Dad's rest schedule. We usually go early, because later in the day he's tired." You'll notice that your parent will have more energy on some days than others, and your awareness of this and your flexibility can help your parent learn to schedule activities accordingly.

Bladder Problems

Bladder problems affect more than three quarters of the people with multiple sclerosis. In healthy people, when the bladder is completely filled with urine a message is sent through the spinal cord to the brain. The brain sends a message back to empty the bladder. In a person with MS the brain may send a message to the bladder before it is completely filled, resulting in frequent trips to the bathroom. Some people experience urgency very frequently and have almost no warning before having to urinate. Often, bladder control can be achieved with medication such as Probanthine, Ditropan, Tofranil, or Levsin.

Another kind of problem occasionally occurs. Some people are unable to empty the bladder completely when they urinate. "Double voiding" can be useful here: after urinating, your parent should wait a few minutes and then try again. Gentle pressure on the bladder may expel more urine. People who experience some urine retention find the medication Baclofen helpful.

Urine retention can lead to bladder infection. Repeated bladder infections can cause kidney damage or bladder or kidney stones. If your parent has frequent bladder infections, a urologist should probably be consulted.

If a large amount of urine constantly remains in the bladder, catheterization may be necessary. This is insertion of a thin rubber or plastic tube through the urethra (the opening through which urine leaves the body) to the bladder, allowing the urine to drain. Catheterization can be uncomfortable at first, but people usually find it an easy skill to master. Using the procedure periodically, according to professional advice, may improve life-style and independence by eliminating excessive trips to the bathroom. It may also result in fewer infections. After a catheter is used for a time, the bladder sometimes resumes normal functioning.

Heather's mother needed to use a catheter but was too nervous to insert it properly. Heather was able to calm and reassure her mother and to insert the catheter for her. Heather's patience helped everyone in the family adjust to their mother's problem. Now outings no longer have to be interrupted by her frequent trips to the bathroom.

Now and then people have a combination of problems: They occasionally have trouble emptying the bladder completely, and they sometimes lose control of urination very easily. A urologist can work out an individual plan to relieve these problems. To guard against occasional accidents, you can buy a variety of thick pads, washable and reusable or disposable diapers, and rubber pants. These items can be found in many drugstores, or look in the Yellow Pages of the telephone directory under "Medical Equipment and Supplies."

In rare cases, a person with MS has no control whatever over the flow of urine. Called incontinence, this frequently occurs when there is bladder infection and ceases when the infection has cleared up. Bladder infections can sometimes be prevented by drinking a lot of fluid when it is convenient to go to the bathroom (especially if your parent is on fluid restriction for better bladder control). Another suggestion is drinking quantities of cranberry juice. Dr. Jack Petajan, professor of neurology and director of the MS Clinic at the University of Utah, advises drinking plentiful fluids, but not beverages containing caffeine. He suggests use of vitamin C, but no more than 500 mg four times a day, taken with food and adequate water.

Something your parent can do with your help is to keep track of time intervals between drinking and urinating over a period of several days. This will help in planning trips and outings, thus benefiting the whole family. You can also encourage your parent to increase the intervals, in order to urinate as infrequently as possible without having an accident.

It is not easy to become attuned to bladder problems; planning when to go to the bathroom is something healthy people don't think about. Try to be supportive and not embarrassed as your parent struggles to overcome this new hurdle.

Vision Difficulties

Almost fifty percent of people with MS have problems with their eyesight at some time, but vision usually returns either on its own or with the help of medication. A serious exacerbation may cause loss of eyesight, which may take two or three months to return. Complete and permanent loss of vision is rare in MS. Robyn Fillman, a vision specialist at Children's Hospital in Columbus, Ohio, is quoted in "Insight into Eyesight" as saying that "even total blindness almost always improves. . . . You will see better on some days than others, because vision is affected by heat, lighting, illness, fatigue, training and your emotional state. But . . . feel confident that you will not lose all of your sight. Most people don't."[3]

Some people's vision does deteriorate, although it may not be MS-related. If your parent has this problem, you can be a real help, as Jessy is. She reads all her father's mail to him and writes out the checks for bills he has to pay. They look forward to this time together, and it has brought them much closer.

Pain

Pain is not one of the main symptoms of MS, although many people who have the disease do experience some pain during their lifetime. Only about ten percent suffer from constant pain, but it is terrifying to experience any pain at all, and it is often mistakenly construed by the person as a worsening of the MS. Dr. Jack Petajan says

---

[3] "Insight into Eyesight" in *Facts & Issues*, June 1989, reprinted from the Fall 1985 issue of *INSIDE MS* (New York: National Multiple Sclerosis Society).

that the site of the pain and its severity have little to do with the seriousness of the multiple sclerosis.

Pain associated with MS can be in the form of pressure, burning, and feelings of pins and needles or tight bands around the body. The effect can range from irritation to severe discomfort. For some people, even brief contact with something soft can result in pain.

The first thing a person so affected should do is consult the doctor, to determine whether the pain is MS-related or not. It may be the result of using different muscles in standing or walking and thus straining them. Walking with weakened legs can sometimes cause back pain. Even sitting in a wheelchair can lead to faulty posture and pain. Your parent should describe the pain to the doctor in as much detail as possible. If the doctor is not helpful, another one should be consulted.

If the pain persists, tranquilizers, antidepressant drugs, and small amounts of Tegretol can relieve some symptoms. Dr. Randall Schapiro advises, in "A Certain Four-Letter Word: Pain,"[4] to try medication first, "because it's the easiest therapy to undertake. If that doesn't work, however, there are nonmedication therapies that sometimes help, such as biofeedback, yoga, hypnosis, and acupuncture." (In addition, meditation, visualization, or physical therapy could be tried.)

Doctors sometimes recommend replacing the pain with another kind of sensation—"pressure, warmth, cold, massage or electrical stimulation." That is what George does. His mother has severe burning in her legs, and he takes icepacks from the freezer and places them where

---

[4] "A Certain Four-Letter Word: Pain" in *Facts & Tissues*, Number 3, reprinted from the Fall 1984 issue of *INSIDE MS* (New York: National Multiple Sclerosis Society), p.2.

the pain is worst. Alice does something different but equally successful. Her father's pain was worst when he was trying to fall asleep. She discovered that reading poetry to him relaxed him, soothed his aches, and enabled him to doze off.

Research into pain is ongoing, and pain control centers are being developed throughout the country. Some of them effectively treat pain with a combination of remedies rather than just one.

Like anything else, it is important not to dwell on negatives when experiencing pain. Help your parent to maintain a positive outlook and an enthusiastic interest in what is going on. Many doctors believe that this attitude helps people not notice their pain as much and feel more in control of their lives.

IF YOUR PARENT MUST BE HOSPITALIZED

No matter how good the care is at home, your parent may occasionally have to be hospitalized. It may be to clear up a bad infection, because of complications from MS, or for other medical reasons. Visit as often as you can and make your parent's stay as pleasant as possible.

Hospitals are usually large, impersonal places, and the one your parent is in may seem very strange to you at first. When you visit, go first to the information desk and find out your parent's floor and room number and how to get there. When you arrive, go directly to the nurses' station and introduce yourself. Ask if there is anything you should be careful about and if it is okay to wake your parent if he or she is asleep. Be sure to knock before you enter the room. Your parent may have a private room or may be sharing the room with other patients. Your parent will probably be wearing a nightgown and a plastic information bracelet. It's best not to sit on the bed; pull up a chair close by. You may want to hold your parent's hand unless he or she is in pain and doesn't want any physical contact. Don't stay too long; thirty to forty-five minutes is about right. If there are other visitors in the room, try to keep the conversation fairly quiet and slow so it won't be confusing for your parent; be sure that he or she is included. He or she may find too much company exhausting and want only immediate family to visit. Be honest with people who ask whether they should go to the hospital.

Nurses and nursing aides are busy people and would welcome your assistance when you are visiting the hospital. There are many things you can do. If your parent can drink ice water, fill up the container and get some straws. Maybe your parent would like a lightweight blanket or an extra pillow. And don't forget to water any flowers or plants in the room. If you can get permission from the nurses or doctor, bring your parent something to eat from a favorite restaurant. Patients in hospitals often get bored with the food, which is usually quite bland. If you are visiting during mealtime, you will notice that it's a hectic time. Your parent would probably appreciate your help. Remove the covers and plastic wrap from the food. Open any canned beverages, and take the cutlery out of its wrapper. Maneuvering in bed is hard to do, so offer to cut the food into bite-sized pieces. Tactfully offer to feed your parent if holding silverware is a problem.

Do your best to keep your parent informed about what is going on at home and in the community. Phone your parent's place of work or social club so you'll have some news for your next visit. If your parent is not having vision problems, bring newspapers, magazines, and books to help fill the long hours when there are no visitors. If your parent cannot see well, you can get large-print books from the library or books-on-tape from your bookstore. A portable tape player (with batteries) and some tapes of music, comedy, or messages from concerned people would probably be very welcome.

Single-Parent Homes

If yours is a single-parent home and you are too young to stay alone, accommodations will be made for you while your parent is hospitalized. If your parents are divorced, perhaps you'll stay with your other parent. Or maybe you can stay with a neighbor, at a friend's house, or with relatives who live near your school. If none of these alternatives are available, there are agencies that can provide someone to come to your home and take care of you. Whatever the situation, it probably won't be as pleasant as being in your own home with your parent there. Be patient; this is only temporary and you'll be back with your parent soon.

Your Reaction

Your parent's stay in the hospital will likely be over soon, and everyone will be back in the familiar routine. At that point you may feel angry at your parent for getting sick and leaving you to go to the hospital. That is not an unusual reaction for you to have, so don't feel that you are callous and unfeeling. Deal with your anger in one of the constructive ways we've discussed elsewhere in this book, or talk about it with someone who will understand.

DOCTORS

Since MS is a chronic disease, you and your family need to have a good working relationship with your parent's doctor. It is important that the doctor be easy to reach, compassionate, and helpful during difficult stages of the disease. If the doctor is not satisfactory in these or other ways, encourage your parent to find another one. Get referrals for neurologists from people you know, especially people with MS, or from your chapter of the MS Society.

You will need to interview several doctors to find one who seems the most compatible. Speak to the doctors over the telephone, and if they sound friendly ask for a brief meeting without being charged a fee. Try to make appointments for the end of the day when the doctors are less busy. Five or ten minutes is all you need to tell whether a doctor seems knowledgeable and caring, with a positive attitude about helping your parent maintain as independent and healthy a life-style as possible. Encourage your parent to communicate directly with the doctor so as to be involved in the healing process.

In addition to your parent's regular doctor, he or she may also benefit from a physician who practices non-traditional medicine. Holistic doctors believe that we are a blend of mind, body, and spirit and that each of these aspects must be treated to improve a patient's health. Doctors who believe in naturopathy use only natural substances in their treatments: sunlight, fresh air, water, and herbs. Doctors who practice osteopathy use traditional medicine but emphasize the connection between body organs and the musculoskeletal system and use their hands to improve structural problems. Other kinds of doctors and various treatments and clinics as well are available. None have been scientifically proven to have any lasting effect on the course of multiple sclerosis, but everyone has the option to try anything they believe will improve their condition. However, no one should abandon traditional medicine entirely. It is ideal to combine various therapies in order to derive the greatest benefit.

WHEN YOUR PARENT IS FEELING BETTER

MS changes almost daily, frequently going from good to bad and back again. Just as your parent is ill today, tomorrow may bring a dramatic improvement. It is difficult to deal with all these ups and downs, but learning to do so is part of the skills that you and your family must master. Your challenge is to find ways to continue doing the things that you enjoy doing together.

If your parent has trouble walking distances, rent a wheelchair and go to a park for an outing in the fresh air or to a shopping mall where there is lots of interesting activity. Numerous movie theaters and auditoriums have special sections for people in wheelchairs and those who accompany them. Phone ahead and check; your parent would probably love to go to a play, a movie, or a concert with you.

Perhaps a celebration is in order and the family can take a trip together. You don't have to go far; just being together in a new and interesting place would be a welcome change. Or maybe your family would like to go somewhere entirely different. Amtrak trains usually have ramps for disabled people, and airplane personnel give excellent help to people who need special attention. If your parent does not normally use a wheelchair and you plan to take a plane, the airlines have wheelchairs for passengers going to and from the plane. Always give notice of your requirements well in advance and phone again just before your trip as a reminder.

Planning a trip is something you can all participate in, whether you are going away for a day, a week, or longer. Once your plans have been finalized, the real work begins—organizing, arranging for handling of the mail, canceling the newspaper and anything else that is delivered regularly, deciding what to take, and finally, packing. There are many things you can do to help your family in getting ready for your excursion and during it as well; keep your eyes and ears open and offer any help you can. As always, your love, caring, and assistance are important and will be appreciated by everyone in your family.

No matter how mild or severe your parent's illness is, you must remain flexible throughout the enormous changes your family life may undergo. You will be faced with frequent choices: Some will be decisions based on the needs of your parent with MS and your family; others will be choices of the heart. If you choose to focus on being helpful and patient rather than withdrawn and critical toward your parent, you will grow into a compassionate, positive person. These qualities will not only ease the stress around you but will be a tremendous asset for you as you enter the adult world. Every moment offers a choice to be positive or negative, and only you can make the final decision—the choice is yours.

CHAPTER ◇ 6

Reflections

Many youngsters grow up with a parent who has a chronic illness. In some homes, it is less difficult than in others because of the differing circumstances and personalities involved. Nevertheless, it is never easy; every day calls for a special effort.

In this chapter some people who have already gone through what you are experiencing share their growing-up years with you. They are now in their thirties or forties, and since their teenage years many treatments have been developed that help to manage MS symptoms. Keep that in mind as they talk about their situations. Although the course of your parent's disease and your family life may be totally different from theirs, you can still gain insight into how others have coped with the challenge of MS.

Mickey's mother was diagnosed with MS when he was twelve years old. His eyes brighten as he expresses his admiration for the strength and courage she has exhibited in dealing with the disease. "She never let her up and down periods get to her, even though she had been very active. She had to cut back on everything; her level of activity decreased. She has always looked for the latest cure and worked hard to stall the symptoms. She fought the progression at every step. But she adapted to each new situation when it became inevitable."

The first couple of years after the diagnosis were confusing for Mickey. He was not told anything about MS, so he tried to ignore it. "Then my parents decided to divorce. MS was one factor among many that Dad was not willing to deal with." Mickey's mother moved out of the house, but he spent all his school breaks with her, and they always maintained close contact.

As he reached his mid-teens, Mickey became a great source of emotional support for his mother, and they "talked about the doubts and concerns she had in dealing with the MS." At first, she didn't tell anyone except her family about the diagnosis. Mickey finally persuaded her to be more open by telling her, "The disease doesn't change who you are; don't hide it any more." She took his advice and they attended an MS support group, which they both found helpful. "Mom began to get involved with the disabled community; I thought that was neat. As I began to be exposed to them, I learned the special problems they deal with. It opened my eyes to the kinds of people they are. They're just like everyone else."

Mickey's experiences and increased awareness probably influenced his decision to study psychology. He also places great emphasis on promoting world peace and tolerance for differences among nations.

Although he has found it hard to watch the physical changes in his mother, it has not altered their relationship. "We are very close and I see her regularly. Rather than just being the child and being cared for, I learned to

REFLECTIONS   ◇ 101

care and take care. I'm glad I've been able to help Mom
and repay her for all the help she has given me."

Mickey feels that the open communication between
him and his mom was the key to getting him through the
tough times. "Everybody gets down. The thing that gets
you out is talking about it. It makes you feel better. When
you feel better, you do better."

Irene's mother was diagnosed in 1949 before any of her
children were born. That was many years ago, but her MS
symptoms have never changed. Says Irene, "She is totally
functional and independent. You'd never know she has
MS by looking at her. She still works and loves to travel.
Nothing stands in her way. She does what she wants to do
to please herself.

"Mom has always accepted the limitations of her MS
and learned to develop a diet and a way of living. She has
a life-style that she can function with. There's never any
apologies. Her two main problems have been her extreme
fatigue and her emotional way of responding to things.
She'll become upset and have crying spells that last
a whole day. Then she'll say, 'Don't bother me' and
hibernate in bed for four or five days. It's difficult to
understand that kind of behavior."

While Irene and her three siblings were growing up,
they all ignored the MS, even though they were told
about it. "It was just there." Still, they noticed when their
mother needed a rest; she would get drawn and tired
looking. Because of her mother's illness and her father's
alcoholism, "There was a lot of chaos in the house. I was
the oldest child. I had to take care of both my parents; I
had to assume a parenting role way too early. I grew up

too fast. I never had a carefree childhood. I never had a childhood at all . . ."

Irene's father left when she was in her late teens. After that some of the tension eased up. Irene finished university and worked for many years as a legal secretary, even while she was married and raising three kids. Now her children are teenagers and she still loves working. She goes to law school three nights a week and in two years will be a lawyer.

In her direct way, Irene talks about the recent closeness she and her mother have developed. It seems to have evolved because Irene now understands her and accepts her as she is. "She hasn't changed. She's still working and independent. Mom is very self-centered. She wants her life to be her own and doesn't like any demands put on her, even if I need her help. I'm disappointed that she has never been interested in her grandchildren. As I was growing up, I used to resent her illness. Now I realize it wasn't her fault. Something good has come out of all this, though. Mom was a good role model. She was ill and without a husband, yet she raised her kids and went on with her life. That's admirable."

Ronald has a B.A. in business management and works in inventory control and sales for an aerospace company. He seems angry as he talks about his father's MS. "Dad started to have trouble walking before the MS diagnosis, but he was stubborn and didn't want help from anyone. After the diagnosis, he was angry at the whole world, but he gradually began to accept help. It's been fourteen years since the diagnosis and Dad's condition has stabilized. He uses a walker to get around and some-times a wheelchair. But his patience is down to zero, and he's irritable and short-tempered.

"After the diagnosis, I wondered, 'Why my family?' I was angry at first but then accepted the fact that my dad was going to be different from everybody else's. It took me two to three years to get over my anger, because I lost out on part of my family life.

"Compared to other people with MS, I guess Dad reacted well. Whenever I suggested the family do some-thing together, he would always say, 'I don't want to impose, but I want to go'. Yet when we got there he always embarrassed me. He was irritable and would make a fool of himself in public. He would say, 'Leave me alone. I can do it myself,' even though he was falling down and needed help."

Ronald is thoughtful for a moment and then continues, "It's been hard to deal with Dad, seeing him unable to do anything to help at home. There's a lot of extra work for Mom. She has to load the wheelchair in and out of the car, help transfer him in and out of bed. . . . They're both retired, and a lot of their income goes for medical supplies."

Ronald now has a full life of his own, but he is a caring and responsible son. "I do all the projects and chores Dad would do if he could. I do the maintenance on the house and car. I painted the house, built a ramp at the front door, repaired the sprinklers in the front yard, and installed the TV antenna on the roof.

"Whenever I'm over there, Dad is bossy and stubborn, but I keep my mouth shut and go along with it. When a parent has MS, you have to be patient and tolerate his behavior. It's not really directed at you."

Jill's dad was diagnosed with MS when he was in his late twenties; she was born four years later. As far back as she can remember, he used a cane. "He used to tell us about falling a lot at work. After a while he started using Canadian crutches, and when I was finishing elementary school he began using a manual wheelchair.

"I remember when he had the use of his arms he played with us. Later on there were no more hugs, and he didn't tuck me into bed anymore. I was sad. I had always been Daddy's girl, and he was my hero. He told us he thought he would die at forty. I was so afraid that sometimes I would cry into my pillow and think, 'What if I wake up and he's dead?'"

But he didn't die; he's well into his sixties and going strong. Although he's a quadriplegic, he works at the same job he's always had. "One muscle in his arm is okay, and he gets around in an electric wheelchair. He uses a pencil to push his dictaphone buttons at work. But he's a really negative person. He yells and complains and is grouchy. He couldn't handle the MS for a while and drank a lot. Mom tried to hide it, but she couldn't. Dad's behavior created a lot of stress on the marriage; however, they're both strong people, and they believe that you marry only once. They knew he had MS when they got married. They've been a real example for us kids."

Jill admires her mother, who stayed home and raised the children. "She's a real caretaker. As soon as I was big enough, I helped her, getting Dad in and out of bed, bringing him stuff he wanted. Before he got the electric wheelchair, I would push him to the car in the morning and help him into it. When I was old enough, I'd drive him to and from work."

Jill found her teenage years the hardest. "I was angry because Dad couldn't hit a baseball around or go backpacking. Then I would feel guilty because it wasn't his fault. I also sometimes resented it because we never went on family vacations like other kids did." Jill was also uncomfortable. "My parents really embarrassed me: Mom was always busy and Dad was in a wheelchair. When you're a teenager you always feel embarrassed by your parents anyway. But still everybody hung out at our house."

She suddenly becomes very serious. "It was hard growing up in the house with Dad. He gets irritated easily and has temper tantrums. He's verbally very abusive and always comes out with put-downs. As a result, my self-esteem really suffered. I wanted to please him so badly that I didn't stand up to him. But when I was halfway through college, my self-esteem suddenly developed. I was tired of letting people take advantage of me. Now I live life the way I want to, not how my parents want me to."

Jill graduated with a liberal arts degree and then got her teaching credentials. Her extreme sensitivity to people with difficulties has made her a better teacher. "I teach in a poor area where drugs and alcohol are part of everyday life. It's a real challenge because the kids need consistency and love. I try to give it." She was recently voted Teacher of the Year at her school because of her successful efforts.

Jill feels that "it is important to let your parent know that you love them, no matter how bad the MS is. Our family didn't express how we felt and were not sensitive to each other's feelings. We didn't talk about MS and that was wrong."

Jill remembers, far back, comparing her family to "the fairy-tale family it was supposed to be. I was angry and blamed my parents. Then I felt guilty because these feelings were directed at the two most important people in my life. I didn't want to admit MS was part of my family—I wanted a perfect family."

When asked what got her through the rough times of growing up, Jill doesn't hesitate. "We lived on a street with good neighbors; there were lots of people taking care of everybody. But most important of all was and still is my involvement with church. I have always felt that God will always be there to watch over you and take care of you."

Anne is an attractive and obviously well-educated woman. When she was four years old, her mother was diagnosed with MS; a few years later she began using a wheelchair. "My mother spoke in a slow, shaky voice, and her head shook badly. She couldn't hold anything and had to be fed. We had a housekeeper to care for her, but I had to take over after school and on weekends. I felt helpless and trapped because I was the only one to do things. I was in charge of the house and did the grocery shopping and housework and cooked the meals. I really had no child-hood. I was shy of my peers and only had one friend.

"I never had a relationship with my mother or saw her as a human being. I saw her as frail, weak, and not very smart. That was probably because my father discounted everything she did and said.

"Dad was an accountant and worked long and hard. We were close; I became his confidante. I always looked to him for guidance and approval, but he never gave me any compliments; he just told me what I had done wrong. He was depressed and angry a lot of the time. He has always felt that he's wonderful and is continually a victim.

"When I was thirteen, Dad and I wanted a family vacation. Since there was no one to take care of my mother, Dad put her in a nursing home. When we got back, we realized it was easier at home without all the commotion she caused, so we left her there. I visited her weekly but hated it because the nursing home was filled with old, ser?le people. My mother was always sweet and passive and smiled a lot. When I was seventeen, she got pneumonia and died a couple of days later.

"I feel guilty now because I wasn't close to my mother and didn't treat her with respect. I also feel guilty because she spent the last four years of her life with old people she couldn't relate to. At that time there were no treatments for MS. Had she lived now, things could have been so much different . . ."

When asked what advice she would give young people in her situation, Anne suggests, "Get whatever support you can from your family and outside. Go to support groups whenever possible. Be open to suggestions from professional caregivers like psychotherapists. Don't feel like a martyr.

"My childhood totally affected my choice of career. I'm a family therapist, and I'm very sensitive to the needs of a family when there's a chronic illness. No feelings were ever expressed in our house, and I grew up unable to discuss my feelings with anyone. It wasn't until I had graduated from university and was attending social work school that I finally learned to express my feelings.

"My husband and I relate well to each other. We have three sons, and I've always tried to give them what I didn't get—attention, positive regard, time, and opportunities for extracurricular interests.

"It was difficult without a mother as a role model. I didn't know how to be feminine. But my childhood has had some good effects on my development. I never allow anyone to manipulate me, and I'm experienced enough to see it coming. I'm independent and self-reliant. I'm a survivor."

Amber is a spunky woman with a zest for life. She has a B.A. degree with a major in cinema and television. Although experienced in all aspects of the performing arts, she is presently making her livelihood as a stuntwoman.

"Dad had MS before I was born and is in good condition for someone having it for so long. He has a really positive outlook on life and takes care of other people with MS by spending hours on the phone with them. Sometimes I get angry because he puts other people before his family, but it makes him feel good to help others, and that's important. He reads widely on MS and tries everything new that might be helpful. He eats well and takes huge doses of vitamins. He exercises every day to help his body and keep himself stress-free.

"Now he's always in the wheelchair. Sometimes we talk about the past, but it's always brief; he never dwells on it. He tells me his dreams, and in a lot of them he is walking."

When thinking about what has been hardest for her to deal with, Amber's eyes fill with tears. "His life is completely different from what it could have been. He used to be a real leader in the community. When he was a doctor, he always gave free services to the poor. Now his realm is smaller; he's just targeting for MS patients. He could have affected more people and more lives."

Amber feels strongly that if one person in the family has MS, it affects everyone. "I believe that young people who have a parent with MS should learn as much as they can about the disease and discuss it with their parents. They can't live in denial. When MS hits, it breaks everyone apart. It's necessary to pull together and work through it together. That is important for everyone's mental health. Strength is an important factor. It's needed to keep the family together.

"I always got support from seeing Mom's strength and realized that's what kept our family together. She's patient and tolerant and takes control of everything. Sometimes I resent it when Dad doesn't acknowledge what she does. I'm very close to Mom and would do anything to protect her."

Amber has learned to tolerate differences. "I understand that everybody goes at their own speed. You have to be patient and reach out to people because you live in the world with other people." From her home life and volunteer work with disabled veterans and homeless people, Amber has developed an acute understanding of the value of life. "Life is a gift. Sometimes it's work, sometimes it's not work. But it's always a gift."

Some of these people have had it relatively easy; others had sad years as they were growing up and now have unhappy memories. All of them, however, developed inner strengths that enabled them to survive. And you will too, no matter how impossible that may seem right now.

As you were reading, you may have noticed how Anne and Jill regretted the lack of communication and sharing of feelings in their homes. On the other hand, Mickey found talking openly with his mother the essential ingredient for his emotional survival. Discussing your feelings is so important for you right now. Being close to someone caring and understanding can make all the difference in the world.

You also need to find something that gives you positive support. It may be sports or excelling at school, a hobby, a competitive game like chess or backgammon, joining a club that does things that give you pleasure, doing volunteer work, or perhaps strengthening your belief in God. Whatever coping mechanisms you use will be uniquely your own and may not be totally understood by your family. That's okay. These outlets will absorb your anger, frustration, or other negative emotions. They will also strengthen your developing character and enable you to surmount anything you have to go through, now or in the future.

CHAPTER 7

Advice From

Other Teens

Even though it may frequently seem as if you're the only one in the world with a disabled parent who is difficult to live with, you are not alone. Many young people are in exactly the same situation, feeling frustrated by unpredictable lives and excessive responsibilities.

Some of the teenagers who have been quoted throughout this book were asked if they had any advice for other teens in similar circumstances. A number of them did, and here it is:

Royal says that after your parent is diagnosed with MS, "it takes a while to sort out your feelings. You may be frightened. It's important to deal with all of your feelings. . . . I accept the fact that nothing can be done and worry would be wasted. I deal with Dad as he is and now enjoy his company more than I used to." He advises,

"Look to sharing time with your parent rather than being uncomfortable because he's different."

Shannon feels it's important to be supportive. "Every day your parent is well, be happy. Most of all, be grateful that your parent is still there with you."

Sean says, "Don't put your parent down. Have patience and empathy for what he or she is going through. Possibly something like this could happen to you."

As a teenager, Courtney says, "We are impressionable and embarrassed by our situation, but it happens to a lot of other families too. If you can't change a situation, accept it and go on from there. I've discovered that people have a lot of respect for the way my family is dealing with MS. They often say that we must be special people to be coping so well. I don't feel that we're special at all. We're just facing what has to be faced."

Raquel says, "I treat Dad like he doesn't have MS."

Frank emphasizes the need for patience. "People with MS go very slowly. You have to help them out as much as you can."

Lee advises helping your parent "if he needs it, because there are lots of things he physically can't do." Seeing the effect of MS on his father, he says, "It gives you a lot of respect for just being able to get around."

In Maria's house, "MS is kind of like a secret." She says, "You should bring it up, even if your parents don't. Try to talk about it, so you know what's going on."

Margo is convinced it's important to "be aware of the MS and be helpful."

James and his father have a much closer relationship since his mother got MS. They sit together and read about the disease and then discuss it. James advises, "Confront the situation. Talk it out. Don't just sit and worry about it. Feel and understand what your parent is going through. Don't concentrate on feeling sorry for yourself by thinking, 'This is so horrible for me' or 'I've lost this and that.' Include your parent in your life as much as possible and treat her like before. Don't feel like she's abandoning you because she's preoccupied with the disease. If it's time for you to go away to school or move out, don't hold your life back. Your parent will understand."

Leslie says: "Have patience and cooperate."

Jessy feels good about the way she treats her father. "I've been his friend. I've been there for him."

In Lynn's opinion, "Young people today just quit if things don't go the way they want." She knows she is often guilty of that herself and finds it hard to keep trying to get along with her father. However, she says, "A lot of patience and respect are necessary when you have a disabled parent."

Kevin says emphatically, "Your parent raised you. You owe everything you have to her, even your life. Try to be patient. She needs your understanding, cooperation, and help. Don't wait until she's eighty years old to give back. There are little things you can do right now, like setting the table, making dinner, even rolling her over in bed. Sometimes your parent's hostility will be directed at you, but you have to be objective and realize it's not your fault your parent is angry. Most important of all, be truthful in telling people how you feel."

Mary has strong regrets about the way MS was handled by her parents. "I wish we had been talked to by both parents. They swept it under the rug." But she says, "Kids with a disabled parent should try to be a little understanding. That's a big thing for a teenager to have to do, but make a real effort."

Thomas says, "It really hits home when someone

close to you gets sick; it's not like when it happens to a stranger. Be understanding and try to keep your parent happy. He or she has no say-so in the situation. Try to motivate your parent to be involved in things. Be thankful you still have your parent. Be happy. Something that's really important is your health."

Lorene advises having "patience, understanding, help, and support."

Harris says, "Teenagers should spend more time understanding and working within their situation to solve the problems; don't rebel against what's happening and create new problems. It's unfair to blame your parent, who had no choice in the matter. It's possible for you to live a normal life. You just have to find the way while working within the limitations MS places on your family."

Erica advises, "Help your parent as much as possible, because it's hard and stressful having the MS." She adds, "Whenever I started getting depressed and feeling sorry for Mom, I'd go in my room and shut off the lights. I'd do that a lot and I did a lot of crying. That's when I'd pray that Mom would get better, that she wouldn't have to go through all this." She also says, "Keep your hopes up. Just have faith. God answered a lot of my prayers."

As for dealing with the MS, Joe suggests, "Take it as it comes." He says, "Dad needs to build his own self-confidence, so I don't try to help him that much." Joe says with conviction, "As much as your parent has supported you in the past, now there's a reversal; be helpful, supportive, and loving."

Heather has gotten a lot of support from talking with her friends. "It's important to be supportive, and because the situation could be worse, you need to enjoy what you have. It's okay to show your feelings. It may hurt your parent at first, but it's really important to do. You're not alone. There are lots of kids in your situation."

David suggests, "Don't forget what your parent was like before the MS—mentally, emotionally, and physically. Mom did lots when we were kids. Even in tough times, we all would go skiing or hiking on weekends. If she could, she'd still be doing these things." He thinks attitude is important. "Don't kowtow to the disease. Keep MS from dominating your attitude to your parent. Don't treat her special because she has MS. Offer extra physical help, but only when it's necessary. Treat her with the same love and respect you always had. Mom has always loved us, and that's given me loyalty to her; she's still my mom and she deserves respect for that." David has a double burden; his brother does not pay attention to their mother. Because of that he advises, "Try to think of your siblings' needs and take some of the weight off them."

What you probably noticed running through all these suggestions is how important it is to be supportive and helpful to your parent when necessary, but always encourage independence in every possible way. These young people feel empathy, loyalty, and a desire to repay their parents for the good years when they were healthy and did so much for their children.

It's tough being a parent at the best of times. With a chronic disease, the job of being a good parent is much more difficult, requiring tremendous energy that ill people often don't have.

Your youth and strength are in sharp contrast to your parent's struggles to maintain some semblance of what life was like before MS. You have your whole life before you. The period you're experiencing now is just a phase—you will get through it and on to other things that will give you a sense of joy and fulfillment. There's a wonderful life waiting for you; meet it with enthusiasm and an open heart and mind.

Appendix

NATIONAL MULTIPLE SCLEROSIS SOCIETY

The National Multiple Sclerosis Society (NMSS) is a multifaceted organization headquartered at 733 Third Avenue, New York, NY 10017–5706. Among its functions are funding research into the cause, prevention, treatment, and cure of multiple sclerosis, and raising money for programs and services.

The Information Resource Center offers an efficient and thorough information service for questions about diagnosis, symptoms, research, available treatments, psychosocial issues, or any other aspects of multiple sclerosis. First phone your local chapter for answers to your questions. If additional information is needed, telephone the national office in New York. The toll-free number, 1 (800) 227-3166, is answered from 11 a.m. to 5 p.m. Eastern Time. It is often busy. If your question is a short one you can call 1 (800) LEARN-MS and leave your question and your name and address on the answering machine, which operates 24 hours a day. (You can also ask for a general information packet about MS.)

The Information Resource Center publishes about thirty pamphlets, most of them free, and a half dozen books that can be purchased. The subjects include mental and emotional health, symptom management, and exercises that can be done by people in various stages of disability. You can request an order form that lists everything available. There is also an extensive bibliography of books published throughout the Western world.

INSIDE MS, a magazine published by the NMSS, is sent to all members every three months. (Membership in the NMSS is free if a person has MS.) It contains informative articles about up-to-date diagnostic methods and research and various treatments for specific symptoms. There are also personal stories in which people with MS describe how they have maintained their independence while dealing with the changes characteristic of the disease.

The NMSS has more than ninety chapters in the United States, affiliated with over seventy clinical facilities that diagnose and treat MS patients, including provision of physical therapy. MS chapters also offer a variety of services within their communities. Not all services are available in every chapter:

- Emergency services: Financial assistance, transportation, and crisis intervention (unscheduled help when something happens in your life that needs immediate attention).
- Activities for teenagers who have a parent with MS: Support groups or pen-pal programs that put you in touch with other teens in your situation.
- Respite care: Programs to give caregivers a break from their day-to-day responsibilities.
- Employment counseling and career guidance for your parent with MS.
- Educational workshops for people with MS and their families.
- Special programs for the newly diagnosed.
- Chapter newsletters containing updates on

research, support services, and chapter activities such as exercise or swimming programs, yoga, and guest speakers at meetings.

- Referrals to doctors and other health professionals.
- A variety of counseling: individual, group, peer, and family. Support groups offer people with MS a chance to get together and share experiences and problems.
- Advocacy for equal access: Chapter-sponsored activities to assure that public places and services are readily accessible to disabled members of a community. This includes ramps in public places, public transportation, health care, and curb-cuts on sidewalks. Emphasis is also placed on equal employment opportunities as well as appropriate services from government agencies.
- Information on where medical or therapeutic equipment can be purchased. Chapters also offer short- or long-term loans for a wide range of equipment.

Still other services are offered by the National Multiple Sclerosis Society. You can obtain further information from your local chapter or the head office in New York.

CHAPTER LIST

ALABAMA
Alabama Chapter
3125 Montgomery Highway
Birmingham, AL 35209
　　　205-879-8881
FAX: 205-870-8726

ALASKA
Alaska Chapter
511 West 41st Avenue
Anchorage, AK 99503
    907-563-1115
FAX: 907-562-6673

ARIZONA
Desert Southwest Chapter
424 East Southern Avenue
Tempe, AZ 85282
    602-968-2488
FAX: 602-966-4049

ARKANSAS
Arkansas Chapter
1100 North University
Evergreen Place
Little Rock, AR 72205
    501-663-6767
FAX: 501-666-4355

CALIFORNIA
Central California Chapter
825 West Ashlan
Clovis, CA 93612-4735
    209-291-7751

Channel Islands Chapter
3022-A De La Vina
Santa Barbara, CA 93105
    805-682-8783

Mountain Valley Chapter
2277 Watt Avenue
Sacramento, CA 95825
    916-486-8981
FAX: 916-486-1190

Northern California Chapter
520 Third Street
Oakland, CA 94607
    510-268-0572
FAX: 510-451-8796

Orange County Chapter
17752 Mitchell
Irvine, CA 92714
    714-752-1680
FAX: 714-833-3104

San Diego Area Chapter
2515 Camino Del Rio South
San Diego, CA 92108
    619-297-4363
FAX: 619-297-6003

Santa Clara County Chapter
2255 Martin Avenue
Santa Clara, CA 95050
    408-988-7557
FAX: 408-988-1816

Southern California Chapter
230 North Maryland Avenue
Glendale, CA 91206-4261
    818-247-1175
FAX: 818-247-1364

COLORADO
Colorado Chapter
1777 South Harrison Street
Denver, CO 80210
    303-691-2956
FAX: 303-758-8349

CONNECTICUT
Greater Connecticut Chapter
74 Batterson Park Road
Farmington, CT 06032
    203-674-1995
FAX: 203-674-0364

Western Connecticut Chapter
83 East Avenue
Norwalk, CT 06851
    203-838-1033
FAX: 203-838-1872

DELAWARE
Delaware Chapter
500 Duncan Road
Wilmington, DE 19809
    302-764-7710
FAX: 302-764-7747

DISTRICT OF COLUMBIA
National Capital Chapter
2021 K Street NW
Washington, DC 20006
    202-296-5363
FAX: 202-296-3425

FLORIDA
Central Florida Chapter
3191 Maguire Blvd
Orlando, FL 32803
    407-896-3873

Florida Gulf Coast Chapter
5420 Bay Center Drive
Tampa, FL 33609-3402
    813-287-2939
FAX: 813-286-9576

North Florida Chapter
One San Jose Place
Jacksonville, FL 32257
    904-262-6767

South Florida Chapter
5410 NW 33rd Avenue
Fort Lauderdale, FL 33309
    305-731-4224
FAX: 305-739-1398

GEORGIA
Georgia Chapter
1365 Peachtree Street NE
Atlanta, GA 30309
    404-874-9797
FAX: 404-874-8453

HAWAII
Hawaiian Islands Chapter
245 North Kukui Street
Honolulu, HI 96817
     808-531-4127
FAX: 808-538-3503

IDAHO
Idaho Chapter
6901 Emerald
Boise, ID 83704
     208-322-6721

ILLINOIS
Chicago-Northern Illinois Chapter
600 South Federal Street
Chicago, IL 60605
     312-922-8000
FAX: 312-922-2752

Greater Illinois Chapter
1703-B West Candletree Drive
Peoria, IL 61614
     309-693-0600

INDIANA
Indiana State Chapter
615 North Alabama Street
Indianapolis, IN 46204
     317-634-8796
FAX: 317-686-0617

IOWA
Iowa Chapter
2400 86th Street
Des Moines, IA 50322
     515-270-6337
FAX: 515-270-0337

KANSAS
Mid-America Chapter
P.O. Box 2292
Shawnee Mission, KS 66201
     913-432-3926
FAX: 913-432-6912

South Central & West Kansas Chapter
1510 West Douglas
Wichita, KS 67203
     316-264-5425

KENTUCKY
Kentucky Chapter
Kosair Charities Centre
982 Eastern Parkway
Louisville, KY 40217
     502-636-1700

LOUISIANA
Louisiana Chapter
2901 Ridgelake Drive
Metairie, LA 70002
     504-832-4013
FAX: 504-831-7188

MAINE
Maine Chapter
P.O. Box 8730
Portland, ME 04104
    207-761-5815
FAX: 207-761-5817

MARYLAND
Maryland Chapter
1055 Taylor Avenue
Towson, MD 21204
    301-821-8626
FAX: 301-821-8030

MASSACHUSETTS
Massachusetts Chapter
400-1 Totten Pond Road
Waltham, MA 02154
    617-890-4990
FAX: 617-890-2089

MICHIGAN
Michigan Chapter
26111 Evergreen
Southfield, MI 48076
    313-350-0020
FAX: 313-350-0029

MINNESOTA
Minnesota North Star Chapter
2344 Nicollet Avenue
Minneapolis, MN 55404
    612-870-1500
FAX: 612-870-0265

MISSISSIPPI
Mississippi Chapter
6055 Highway 18 South
Jackson, MS 39209
   601-922-7979
FAX: 601-922-8048

MISSOURI
Gateway Area Chapter
915 Olive Street
St. Louis, MO 63101
   314-241-8285
FAX: 314-241-8836

MONTANA
Montana Chapter
600 Central Plaza
Great Falls, MT 59401
   406-452-9529

NEBRASKA
Midlands Chapter
538 Elkwood Mall—The Center
42nd & Center Streets
Omaha, NE 68105-2982
   402-345-9026

NEVADA
Great Basin Sierra Chapter
3100 Mill Street
Reno, NV 89502
   702-329-7180

NEW HAMPSHIRE
New Hampshire Chapter
50 Bridge Street
Manchester, NH 03101
    602-623-3501

NEW JERSEY
Bergen-Passaic Counties Chapter
P.O. Box 348
730 River Road
New Milford, NJ 07646-3032
    201-967-5599
FAX: 201-967-7085

Mid-Jersey Chapter
801 Belmar Plaza
Belmar, NJ 07719
    908-681-2322
FAX: 908-681-2341

Northern New Jersey Chapter
60 South Fullerton Avenue
Montclair, NJ 07042-2681
    201-783-6441
FAX: 201-746-6207

NEW MEXICO
Rio Grande Chapter
P.O. Box 80675
Albuquerque, NM 87198-0675
    505-842-6767
FAX: 505-842-0055

NEW YORK
Capital District Chapter
421 New Karner Road
Albany, NY 12205
       518-452-1631
FAX: 518-452-1636

Greater Broome County Chapter
67 Main Street
Binghamton, NY 13905
       607-724-5464

Long Island Chapter
33 Walt Whitman Road
Huntington Station, NY 11746
       516-421-3857
FAX: 516-421-3929

New York City Chapter
30 West 26th Street
New York, NY 10010-2094
       212-463-7787
FAX: 212-989-4362

Rochester Area Chapter
1000 Elmwood Avenue
Rochester, NY 14620
       716-271-0801
FAX: 716-442-7573

Southern New York Chapter
11 Skyline Drive
Hawthorne, NY 10532
       914-345-3500
FAX: 914-345-3504

Upstate New York Chapter
224 Harrison Street
Syracuse, NY 13202
   315-422-1447

Western New York/NW Pennsylvania Chapter
2060 Sheridan Drive
Buffalo, NY 14223
   716-875-7710

NORTH CAROLINA
Eastern North Carolina Chapter
3725 National Drive
Raleigh, NC 27612-4879
   919-781-0676

Central North Carolina Chapter
2302 West Meadowview Road
Greensboro, NC 27407-3700
   919-299-4136
FAX: 919-855-3039

Greater Carolinas Chapter
1515 Mockingbird Lane
Charlotte, NC 28209
   704-525-2955
FAX: 704-527-0406

NORTH DAKOTA
Dakota Chapter
2801 Main Avenue
Fargo, ND 58103
   701-235-2678
FAX: 701-232-5780

OHIO
Mid-Ohio Chapter
1550 Old Henderson Road
Columbus, OH 43220
     614-459-2220
FAX: 614-459-2929

Northeast Ohio Chapter
3101 Euclid Avenue
Cleveland, OH 44115
     216-391-6700

Northwest Ohio Chapter
1023 North Reynolds Road
Toledo, OH 43615
     419-531-1671
FAX: 419-531-2733

Southwest Ohio/Northern Kentucky Chapter
Park Lane Apartments
4201 Victory Parkway
Cincinnati, OH 45229
     513-281-5200
FAX: 513-281-5162

Western Ohio Chapter
Woolpert Building
409 East Monument
Dayton, OH 45402
     513-461-5232

OKLAHOMA
Oklahoma Chapter
2745 East Skelly Drive
Tulsa, OK 74105
    918-747-9458
FAX: 918-744-6085

OREGON
Oregon Chapter
5901 SW Macadam
Portland, OR 97201
    503-223-9511
FAX: 503-223-2912

PENNSYLVANIA
Allegheny District Chapter
1040 Fifth Avenue
Pittsburgh, PA 15219
    412-261-6347
FAX: 412-391-8144

Central Pennsylvania Chapter
2209 Forest Hills Drive
Harrisburg, PA 17112-1005
    717-652-2108
FAX: 717-652-2590

Greater Delaware Valley Chapter
117 South 17th Street
Philadelphia, PA 19103
    215-963-0100
FAX: 215-963-0335

Lancaster County Chapter
117 D South West End Avenue
Lancaster, PA 17603
    717-397-1481

PUERTO RICO
Puerto Rico Chapter
P.O. Box 13605
Santurce, PR 00908
    809-798-8043

RHODE ISLAND
Rhode Island Chapter
535 Centerville Road
Warwick, RI 02886
    401-738-8383
FAX: 401-738-8469

SOUTH CAROLINA
South Carolina Chapter
2711 Middleburg Drive
Columbia, SC 29204
    803-799-7848

TENNESSEE
Middle Tennessee Chapter
2200 21st Avenue South
Nashville, TN 37212
    615-269-9055

Mid-South Chapter
P.O. Box 241988
Memphis, TN 38124-1988
    901-763-3601
FAX: 901-763-2907

Setenga Chapter
P.O. Box 3331
Chattanooga, TN 37404-3331
    615-624-2064

TEXAS
North Texas Chapter
8214 Westchester Drive
Dallas, TX 75225
    214-373-1400
FAX: 214-373-7200

Panhandle Chapter
715 South Lamar
Amarillo, TX 79106
    806-372-4429
FAX: 806-372-6421

Southeast Texas Chapter
2211 Norfolk
Houston, TX 77098
    713-526-8967
FAX: 713-526-4049

South Texas Chapter
4204 Woodcock Drive
San Antonio, TX 78228
    512-735-9366
FAX: 512-734-7073

Tri-Cities of Texas Chapter
6001 Bridge Street
Fort Worth, TX 76112
    817-496-4475

West Texas Chapter
P.O. Box 4636
Midland, TX 79704
    915-699-7787
FAX: 915-699-7789

UTAH
Utah State Chapter
525 South 300 West
Salt Lake City, UT 84101
    801-575-8500

VERMONT
Vermont Chapter
Champlain Mill #42
1 Main Street
Winooski, VT 05404
    802-655-3666

VIRGINIA
Blue Ridge Chapter
P.O. Box 6808
Charlottesville, VA 22906
    804-971-8010

Central Virginia Chapter
5001 West Broad Street
Richmond, VA 23230
    804-282-2358

Hampton Roads Chapter
405 South Parliament Drive
Virginia Beach, VA 23462
    804-490-9627

WASHINGTON
Central Washington Chapter
P.O. Box 1093
Yakima, WA 98907
    509-248-2350

Inland Northwest Chapter
East 818 Sharp
Spokane, WA 99202
    509-482-2022

Western Washington Chapter
2328 6th Avenue
Seattle, WA 98121
    206-728-1088
FAX: 206-728-4397

WEST VIRGINIA
West Virginia Chapter
P.O. Box 3064
Charleston, WV 25331
    304-342-5295

WISCONSIN
Wisconsin Chapter
615 East Michigan
Milwaukee, WI 53202
    414-276-4606
FAX: 414-276-5848

WYOMING
Wyoming Chapter
P.O. Box 556
Casper, WY 82602
    307-234-2340

MULTIPLE SCLEROSIS SOCIETY OF CANADA

Canada has one of the highest rates of multiple sclerosis in the world. As a result, the Multiple Sclerosis Society of Canada conducts public awareness programs to make all Canadians more knowledgeable about the disease. The Society also raises money to fund many programs, such as services and information for people with MS and their families and research into the cause, prevention, treatment, and cure of MS.

When you call the toll-free number in Canada, 1 (800) 268-7582, it rings at the division office in the province you are calling from. If desired, you will be given the address and telephone number of your nearest chapter. Confidentiality is respected. If you *request*, information about MS can be sent to you in a plain envelope and you will not be contacted any further.

There are thirteen clinics across the country that diagnose, assess, and make recommendations for ongoing medical care. Clinical services are free because the government provides basic health services. When needed, MS clinics make referrals to other services. They occasionally offer patients the opportunity to participate in research projects such as testing new medications or treatments.

Besides the division offices and clinics, there are more than one hundred twenty chapters. Services offered differ from chapter to chapter but may include:

- Counseling on an individual or family basis, one-to-one peer support, special programs for the newly diagnosed, and support and self-help groups.
- Regular lectures and workshops for people who have MS and their families.

- Booklets about MS, occasional workshops, and support groups for teens who have a parent with MS.
- Many pamphlets and books about MS are free or can be borrowed from division offices. *MS Canada* is a magazine containing articles about the latest research, new ways of diagnosing MS, personal stories of people who deal effectively with the disease, and society activities. The magazine is published every three months; members receive it automatically.
- A variety of exercise, social, and recreational activities for individuals or families are offered by the chapters, such as swimming, yoga, tai chi, riding for the disabled, and crafts.
- Respite care is not available through the MS Society, but information is available on where it can be obtained.
- In some regions of the country, the government helps fund the purchase of necessary equipment such as wheelchairs, walkers, and canes. Where government or insurance help is unavailable, the MS Society may help with the cost of its purchase. In addition, mobility equipment can be borrowed from many division offices and chapters.
- The MS Society supports social action to help integrate people disabled by MS into the community. The main focus of their efforts is directed toward public transportation, curb-cuts, and accessibility to public buildings. The Society is working to bring about change in regulations concerning private insurance and government pensions to make them more available to the disabled.

• Home visiting and telephone contact are often available.

Membership in the Multiple Sclerosis Society of Canada is free for anyone with MS. All of its programs and services are too numerous to be listed. Call your division office and find out exactly what is happening where you live.

DIVISION OFFICES

National Office
250 Bloor Street East
Toronto, Ontario M4W 3P9
        (416) 922-6065
FAX: (416) 922-7538

Alberta
11203 – 70th Street
Edmonton, Alta. T5B 1T1
        (403) 471-3313
FAX: (403) 479-2286

Atlantic
45 Alderney Drive
Dartmouth, N.S. B2Y 2N6
        (902) 465-7251
FAX: (902) 469-7490

British Columbia
6125 Sussex Avenue
Burnaby, B.C. V5H 4G1
        (604) 437-3244
FAX: (604) 437-3020

Manitoba
825 Sherbrook Street
Winnipeg, Manitoba R3A 1M5
(204) 783-8585
FAX: (204) 774-6457

Ontario
250 Bloor Street East
Toronto, Ontario M4W 3P9
(416) 922-6065
FAX: (416) 922-7538

Quebec
279, rue Sherbrooke ouest
Montreal, Quebec H2X 1Y2
(514) 849-7591
FAX: (514) 849-8914

Saskatchewan
2329 – 11th Avenue
Regina, Sask. S4P 0K2
(306) 522-5607
FAX: (306) 565-0477

Vancouver Island
1004 North Park Street
Victoria, B.C. V8T 1C6
(604) 388-6496

For Further Reading

Benedict, Helen. *Safe, Strong & Streetwise*. Boston & Toronto: Joy Street Books—Little, Brown and Company, 1987.

Berkus, Rusty. *Life Is a Gift*. Los Angeles: Red Rose Press, 1982.

France, Kenneth. *The Hospital Patient, A Guide for Family and Friends*. Carlisle, PA: New Day Publishers, 1987.

Gardner, James E., Ph.D. *The Turbulent Teens*. Los Angeles: Sorrento Press, Inc., 1983.

Gawain, Shakti. *Creative Visualization*. San Rafael, CA: New World Library, 1978.

Graham, Judy. *Multiple Sclerosis—A Self-help Guide to Its Management*. Wellingborough, Northamptonshire, NN8 2RQ England: Thorsons Publishers Limited, 1987.

Griffin, Moira. *Going the Distance*. New York: E.P. Dutton, 1989.

Kolodny, Nancy J., M.A., M.S.W.; Kolodny, Robert C., M.D., and Bratter, Thomas E., Ed.D. *Smart Choices*. Boston: Little, Brown and Company, 1986.

Lechtenberg, Richard, M.D. *Multiple Sclerosis Fact Book*. Philadelphia: F.A. Davis Company, 1988.

Le Shan, Eda. *When a Parent Is Very Sick*. Boston/Toronto: Joy Street Books—Little, Brown and Company, 1986.

Le Shan, Lawrence, Ph.D. *How to Meditate*. New York: Bantam Books, 1988.

Levine, Stephen. *A Gradual Awakening*. New York: Doubleday, 1989.

Rosner, Louis J., M.D., and Ross, Shelley. *Multiple Sclerosis—New Hope and Practical Advice for People With MS and Their Families*. New York: Prentice-Hall Press, 1987.

Scheinberg, Labe C., M.D., and Holland, Nancy J., M.A., R.N., eds. *Multiple Sclerosis: A Guide for Patients and Their Families.* New York: Raven Press, 1987.

Shuman, Robert Dr, and Schwartz, Janice Dr. *Understanding Multiple Sclerosis: A New Handbook for Families.* New York: Charles Scribner's Sons, 1988.

Soll, Robert W., M.D., Ph.D., and Grenoble, Penelope B., Ph.D. *MS: Something Can Be Done and You Can Do It.* Chicago: Contemporary Books, 1984.

Swank, Roy Laver M.D., Ph.D., and Dugan, Barbara Brewer. *The Multiple Sclerosis Diet Book.* New York: Doubleday, 1987.

Index